GREENLIGHT YOUR TECH CAREER

Beginner's Guide to Self-Taught
Programming After the AI Revolution and
Getting Hired Fast Without a Degree
Through Real-World Coding Experience

Dan Maskins

To *my* beloved wife,
whose love and unwavering support
stand as the greatest **Victory** of my life.
And to my precious daughter,
my entire **World**,
whose laughter brings **Peace**
and fills our days
with endless joy.

If you enjoy this book,
*please think about **sharing** it with others*
who might love it as well

*and leaving a **review**.*
It makes a big difference!

Contents

INTRODUCTION

B eep, beep… beeeee… The heart monitor's relentless alarm pierces the sterile silence, echoing the frantic fight for life. The patient's chest lies open, revealing a still heart where moments ago it pulsed with rhythm. You glance down at your hands. The once-white gloves are smeared crimson and stained with blood. Every breath hitch, a struggle against the suffocating mask. Eyes meet yours – the surgical team's unspoken question hangs heavy in the air.

The clock ticks. A life teeters on the brink. And you… you must decide. By the time you reach this point in surgery, you've dedicated years to education and training. Hours upon hours spent in school, college, medical school, and then residency honing your skills. You've persevered through grueling exams and countless nights on call. All those years led you to this moment.

That's why you could never casually "try" to be a surgeon. The path to becoming a surgeon is a grueling one, demanding years of dedication and sacrifice. But what if I told you that the world of software development is different? Here, you can jump right in and start building real things today without needing years of up-front investment. I'm not talking about writing a "Hello World" program that nobody cares about – a skill you'd find in any other introductory course online. Think of this book as your defibrillator. It's designed for rapid action to bypass the slow, conventional paths and jumpstart your journey into software development. You'll see how it feels to make real changes in working software products, giving you the taste of a developer's life and the skills to land your dream job in this exciting field. This book is your practical guide, ensuring you're equipped with the right tools and knowledge to succeed.

Don't waste your time on outdated curriculums. This book isn't about quick-fix boot camps, either. We'll embrace the cutting-edge, leveraging the power of AI to give you an advantage. This means learning faster and building relevant projects that matter. But don't let change scare you. This book equips you with the adaptable problem-solving and self-learning skills you need to thrive in the ever-evolving world of software development.

Remember that frantic fight for life, the sickening feeling of something precious on the brink of being lost? But what if, instead of a heart on the table, it's your potential wasting away? Does your current situation leave you bored and uninspired, with no time or energy left to explore your potential in software development? Is the idea of a long traditional education path holding you back from pursuing a fulfilling career?

We'll chart your course, showing you what to expect and helping you decide if this game suits you. You'll gain the essential skills – technical and beyond. We will address imposter syndrome, help you select the most suitable tech stack for you, and guide you on how to land your first job with a standout resume, even if you have no commercial software development experience.

This book will reignite the spark, the one that used to make you excited about the future. With every step you take on this journey, feel the rhythm of your new life begin – a steady beat signaling the exciting possibilities ahead. It's not about learning to code; it's about transforming your life and career from an observer to an active participant in the world of software development.

PART I
The Game

WAKE-UP CALL

A sharp beep jolts you awake. It is not the steady cadence of a heart monitor but a digital alarm that is insistent and shrill. Bleary-eyed, you fumble for the source, the sound pulsating through your small apartment, mirroring the dull ache building behind your eyes. Glancing out the window, the cityscape shimmers in the harsh dawn light, a vast grid of buildings and streets. But today, it's not just a city. It's a sprawling open-world game laid out before you. A game you can no longer just observe. This is Software Development City, your new arena, and the beep that woke you was the starting bell. The quest to become a developer has begun.

This city hums with a unique energy. Around you, the faint flicker of screens and the rhythmic tapping of keyboards blend into a symphony of creation. You're not a mere NPC[1] in this world, blindly following predetermined paths. You're the main character, the decision-maker, and the problem-solver. But like any bustling city, this one has its dangers. The constant flood of new information threatens to overwhelm you, making you question your direction. Frustration gnaws at you as progress stalls – a

---

[1] https://en.wikipedia.org/wiki/Non-player_character

digital traffic jam in the city's arteries. And always, there's the nagging question: is this the right path for you? The main quest, of course, is a job – a role with purpose, a team to be a part of. You glimpse potential destinations – the towering skyscrapers of Big Tech, the vibrant storefronts of promising startups, and even the freedom of a nomadic freelance life. The city beckons.

As you take in this vista, you understand the game's first rule: to become a developer, you must think like one. This isn't a quest waiting for an NPC to grant you a title. It's about taking control of your character's development – picking side quests, crafting your first programs, and joining guild-like communities of fellow developers.

Soon, you'll begin this journey of transformation. Each commit will serve as a save point in your journey, and every project will represent a level completed. Your tools will evolve from traditional coding into modern AI-assisted development, but the core gameplay will remain the same: solving problems, building solutions, and leveling up. As you navigate this vast open-world game, you won't just play to win; you will play to transform. The city will watch, and somewhere in those gleaming towers, your future team will be waiting for you. This book will guide you through every step of this exciting adventure.

GAME TUTORIAL

T he screen flickers to life, the familiar cityscape of Software Development City replaced by a series of stark, geometric shapes. "Warning: Game Tutorial starting," a disembodied voice announces, cutting through the soft hum of your computer fan. This... wasn't something mentioned in the guidebooks. You feel a bead of sweat forming on your brow. Is this just a fancy intro or an unexpected test of your skills?

"Welcome, new player," the tutorial voice, your guide in this journey, continues. "Here, there are no easy paths. You must make choices, and those choices will shape your journey." The screen blinks, and a crudely drawn map unfolds. "Think of this level as a survival guide for Software Development City, a glimpse at the obstacles that trip up the unwary."

The map is split into distinct sections, each labeled with a familiar transportation metaphor: walking, city bus tour, taxi, and train. Your pulse quickens. You've heard snippets about these paths, but mostly in arguments, each advocate is confident they've found the right way.

A pixelated figure appears on the map, struggling with a giant, overflowing backpack. "This," the voice proclaims dryly, "is the self-taught journey. Freedom, yes, but with a price." The lone walker is surrounded by a maze of paths, darting this way and that, energy-depleting as the backpack grows heavier.

The map shifts and the walker is now crammed into a bus packed with other excited faces. "The Bootcamp!" the voice announces. "Structure and camaraderie, but remember, the scenery is curated." The bus deposits its passengers with matching certificates and confused expressions at a predetermined destination.

Another pixelated figure climbs into a gleaming yellow taxi. "The coveted internship," the voice explains. "Direct access to the inner workings of the city, invaluable... if you can get a ride." The scene pans out to reveal hundreds of other figures, all competing for the same taxi. The taxi circles the block, its *"Available"* sign flickering tantalizingly, but for every lucky passenger, dozens are left waiting in the rain.

Finally, the map zooms in on a majestic train. "The University Degree," the voice declares. It is the tried-and-true path, a promise of prestige... but expensive, and with schedules not of your own making." The train moves steadily but slowly, never veering from its pre-laid tracks.

As you absorb these options, a question burns in your mind. Unable to contain your curiosity any longer, you blurt out, "Wait, where are the cars? Can't I just drive a car and go wherever I need to in no time?"

The tutorial voice pauses, and you swear you can hear a hint of amusement in its digital tone. "Ah, the allure of cars. They're for experienced drivers, player. You can't just sit in a car and go wherever you want. You must become a driver first, know the road rules, and understand how traffic lights work."

The voice grows more serious. "Did you know that cars have a higher mortality rate than many other modes of transportation? While the specific statistics vary depending on many factors, road traffic accidents are a leading cause of death worldwide!"

Suddenly, the screen shifts, and you find yourself in the driver's seat of a sleek, virtual car. The engine purrs beneath you,

Greenlight Your Tech Career

and the open road stretches ahead. Your hands grip the wheel, knuckles white with anticipation.

The tutorial voice continues in its grave tone: "Picture this: You're on a highway, passing a large semi-truck. You misjudge the distance as you merge back." In that instant, everything changes. The world blurs as your car enters a skid. Tires screech against asphalt. The acrid smell of burning rubber fills your nostrils. Your body tenses, bracing for impact. Time slows to a crawl, each millisecond stretching into eternity.

Then, as quickly as it began, the vision ends. You're back in the tutorial, your breath coming in short, sharp gasps. The memory of the crash feels visceral and real, though you know it was just a simulation. Your hands shake as you reach for the controls.

The tutorial voice, now gentler, breaks the tense silence. "One second of distraction, one moment of overconfidence, and it's over. Experience and knowledge of the rules come first. Then, and only then, can you drive safely."

You nod, still shaken by the intensity of the experience. "I... I understand," you manage to say, your voice barely above a whisper.

"Good," the tutorial responds with a note of approval. "Now, let's return to the paths available to you in Software Development City. Remember, each has its advantages and challenges. Your task is to navigate them wisely."

The cityscape of Software Development City reappears, but you see it with new eyes. The paths ahead may be challenging, but you're ready to face them, one step at a time. After all, in this city, the journey is just as important as the destination.

TICKET TO NOWHERE?

You're late! A surge of panic prickles your skin as you race up the steps of the towering train station, your backpack slamming against your back. You'd imagined your journey into Software Development City starting differently... maybe calmly exploring options, not this breathless dash for a departing train. Glancing at the clock confirms your worst fear – only minutes before the University Degree Express departs. Your heart pounds with each step – this train represents four years of your life and a significant investment. Can you afford to miss it?

You push through a throng of fellow passengers, their diplomas clutched like talismans. The air is heavy with the scent of old paper, a palpable nervous energy buzzing just beneath the surface. Inside the train car, it's a whirlwind. Each seat seems to hold two or three students, textbooks spilling into the aisles. This journey is undeniably popular, but is it the right one for you?

As you wedge into a cramped seat, the muffled conversations swirling around you become a blur. Everyone is debating arcane concepts: Big-O notation, esoteric languages, things you've only vaguely heard of. An icy knot forms in your stomach. Will you ever catch up? The train lurches forward, and out the window, the cityscape of practical projects and job listings you long to explore blurs past. The feeling of being left behind is overwhelming.

The train slows for what feels like hours, maybe days later (time feels warped inside this academic bubble). You disembark, stiff and a bit dizzy. You were promised this train would take you to the heart of Software Development City. But this station... it's on the outskirts. Functional, but gray. Employers swarm a gleaming taxi stand, but their eyes pass right over the crowd of graduates. One student, bolder than the rest, taps someone on the shoulder, shoving a resume forward. The rejection comes before they even finish speaking, a stark reminder of the grim reality of the industry.

Across the station, a single person stands apart, a gleaming yellow taxi pulling up beside them. They climb in without a fuss, leaving you and your fellow graduates staring after them. You heard whispers around you... something about an internship landed during their final year. Luck? Connections? Or was their path different from yours right from the start?

As the taxi speeds off, you're left to ponder. Was the University train a mistake? No... it taught you valuable things. But what this station lacks is clear: a connection to those bustling avenues where software is built, not just dissected. Theory, you realize, is only one piece of the puzzle.

The station begins to fade like a dream sequence, and the familiar voice of your Tutorial Guide breaks through: "Welcome back!" The cheerful voice startles you from your reverie... "See the challenge? The academic train gives you tools, but sometimes those tools aren't what employers are looking for at this moment."

"But" it continues, "Don't write off the station completely. Those with degrees are respected, but respect only gets you so far. Come back here when you have a project under your belt... they might look at you differently."

The station fades from view. You realize one crucial thing: whether you choose a train, a taxi, or even walking, Software Development City is about adapting, returning to those you've met along the way, and always seeking the edge.

"Next on the Tutorial Map," the voice announces, "is the City Bus Tour. Think of it as the Bootcamp route. Let's see if that's more your speed..."

BEYOND THE BUS
WINDOW

The Tutorial fades, replaced by the interior of a crowded bus. You jostle for space, trying to find a seat between the eager faces of other aspiring developers. The smell of stale pastries and nervous sweat hangs in the air. This is the City Bus Tour, the Bootcamp route. It promises speed, a structured path straight to your software development dreams. But is the view really worth the high-ticket price?

The bus lurches forward, and a cheerful instructor starts speaking into a mic. "Welcome, new coders! This tour will be fast paced, a whirlwind journey past the hottest tech!" Out the window, you spot landmarks: HTML District, JavaScript Avenue, and even a glimpse of the intimidating AI Gardens. You and the others pull out your phones, snapping quick photos and making notes, though you already sense there won't be time to revisit them.

"Remember," the instructor's voice cuts through your daze, "This isn't about understanding the history of each landmark. This is about what employers need right now." Your stomach flips. That's the appeal of the bootcamp, but... is keeping up the only thing that matters?

The days become a blur of lessons, projects, and frantic Googling to fill your knowledge gaps. The other passengers (your classmates) become a mix of allies and rivals. You work together late into the night but know you'll all compete for the same few jobs when the tour ends.

The bootcamp, as promised, consumes your life. It's thrilling but exhausting. You realize you're learning to follow directions, not honestly think like a developer. The curriculum speeds past exciting side streets, promising, "We'll come back to that if there's time." But you know, deep down, there never is.

One afternoon, the bus screeches to a halt. The tour is over, and you're deposited back where you started. You blink in the harsh sunlight, clutching your certificate and scrolling through your photo gallery. Like any tourist's vacation snapshots, the images already feel distant and meaningless – landmarks captured but never truly explored, concepts photographed but never deeply understood.

"Don't worry!" trills the disembodied Tutorial voice. "Many new devs start here. You got a taste. Now, the trick is turning it into a meal." It suggests seeking mentors, taking on freelance projects, or even returning to the University station now that you know more about the city's layout.

Suddenly, you spot two familiar faces in the crowd: recent university graduates, their unused diplomas still fresh in their backpacks. They're here seeking practical skills their theoretical education didn't provide. You realize the bootcamp wasn't a wrong choice, but perhaps it's just one piece of a giant puzzle like every other path in Software Development City.

"Next stop," the Tutorial announces, "is self-study, the 'Walking' route. Think of it as wandering the city on your own. Slower, maybe scarier at first... but with the freedom to truly learn the side streets, no tour bus will ever take you down."

LOST IN THE MAZE

The world around you dissolves. The train, the bus, the station… all gone. You find yourself standing on a scenic overlook, the cityscape of Software Development looming vast and unknowable before you. You're suddenly, unmistakably alone in this sprawling metropolis.

This is it, the walking path – the route of self-study. The freedom is exhilarating… and utterly terrifying. People brush past you on either side, their heads down, lost in their journeys. They huddle in tight groups, laughing and talking in rapid code you barely understand, exchanging what sounds like secrets of a language you're still trying to piece together. You take a few hesitant steps, hoping to catch a fragment of their knowledge, but the groups keep moving, conversations fading, leaving you just as unsure of where to start as before.

Your chest tightens with a familiar ache, a mixture of frustration and aimlessness that followed you into this city. You were hoping for an escape – a structured path to a new way of life. But now, even the game seems to offer only more of the same paralysis of choice and isolation.

Days turn into weeks. A weathered map appears in your shaking hand, but it's no beacon of hope. It's more a collection of scribbled notes than any real guide, filled with arrows that lead nowhere and faded warnings about dead-end tech. With a jolt, you realize these are your notes, cobbled together from tutorials, forums, and half-remembered YouTube videos. This chaos is your path. Whenever you think you understand something, you turn another virtual corner and realize how little you know.

One night, as the city buzz fades, silence wraps around you. You look up to find yourself in a dimly lit corner, the buildings here familiar, the ground littered with broken code and discarded side projects. It hits you then: not only are you lost, but you've been going in circles, revisiting the same mistakes over and over.

The tutorials in your bookmarks folder seem to mock you with their promises of quick results and mastery in mere weeks. Each one is another breadcrumb that has led you back here, no closer to understanding than when you started. Frustration bubbles up as you sift through them again, each promising a secret formula, an easy path to expertise that never materializes. This whole time, you realize you've been waiting for magic solutions to carry you forward as if knowledge alone could build your path.

Then, as if a weight shifts, it hits you: all this time, you've been trying to learn without building. You've been caught in an endless loop of tutorials and forums, accumulating facts without shaping them into anything tangible. All this time, you've been consuming ideas but haven't created anything.

You need to build something real – a project of your own. But as the idea settles, a cold wave of realization follows: you don't have the practical skills to bring even a simple project to life. Your knowledge is mostly theoretical, scattered bits and pieces from different sources that you don't know how to fit together.

Your basics might be enough to start with some guidance. What you need isn't more self-study but real experience – somewhere to learn by doing and making mistakes. A small job could let you try out your knowledge and address any gaps. You may not feel ready, but no one truly does. By dawn, as the city glows, you decide to seek an entry-level role to learn and apply yourself. Your foundations might be sufficient for now; you need experience, however imperfect, and the only way to gain it is by taking a chance to leap.

Just then, a triumphant fanfare blares as a familiar voice return. "Congratulations!" it booms. "You've successfully completed the self-study path! You've faced challenges, navigated uncertainty, and emerged as a stronger, more resourceful developer. Now, go forth and conquer the world… with the power of… well, you've got the basics down, right?"

The fanfare sputters and dies out. An awkward silence hangs in the air. You stare, dumbfounded, at the spot where the voice originated. Basics down? Is this some kind of cruel joke?

VICIOUS CYCLE

The flickering holo-display of the quest board mocked you with its cheerful icons and promises of adventure. "Level 70 experience for 'easy' jobs?" Anger surges through you, a bitter taste in your mouth. You scoff at the quest board, the glowing promises of a friendly work environment and cutting-edge tech feeling like outright lies. "The system is rigged," you mutter, echoing the complaints you've seen on online forums in hushed whispers in coffee shops.

The air crackles with tension. You're not alone in this. Beside you are other players, their faces reflecting your frustration. "I spent years on that degree," one laments, their avatar trembling with barely contained rage. "All for this?" Their words echo your own thoughts, a chorus of shared disappointment.

Another player, one who chose the self-teaching route, sighs. "Tutorials are useless. None of them taught me how to build a real-world thing." Everyone nods. The quest board might as well be in a different language.

Disgusted, you turn and walk out of the crowded "Recruitment Outpost." The air inside is thick with discontent, players huddling in small groups, scrolling through impossible job descriptions. Each word – Agile, DevOps, full stack – digs into you, reminders of skills you were somehow supposed to have acquired. You wonder, bitterly, where you were supposed to learn all this.

The corporations behind these impossible quests? They benefit from the churn, picking up those with the elusive "experience" everyone needs. It's a vicious cycle, a game where your struggle feeds their need for cheap labor.

It hits you like a rogue monster attack: It's a feature, not a bug! University, bootcamps, even those "helpful" YouTube tutorials... they're all part of a cycle, churning out just enough knowledge to be worthless but not enough to be employable. A trap hidden in plain sight.

Your frustration boils over. "This isn't right," you growl, attracting curious glances from nearby players. You don't care. All those guides had promised a clear path, but the reality is nothing like they said. The tutorials were a lie, promising you a path that doesn't exist.

But just as despair settles over you like a suffocating fog, a soft meow catches your attention. A small, white cat appears beside you, its eyes glowing with an otherworldly light. It rubs against your leg, purring insistently. A system notification flashes across your screen: *"Quest Helper Plugin has been installed. Proceed to Inventory to activate."*

Startled, you look around. No one else seems to see the cat. It sits down, its tail twitching expectantly. With a mix of curiosity and skepticism, you reach down to pet it. As your hand touches its soft fur, information floods your mind: the cat is the Quest Helper, a digital companion designed to guide you through this broken system.

Confused, you navigate to your inventory backpack, a cluttered mess of notes and outdated gear. It looks like your real-world desk, honestly. And then you see the book representing the Quest Helper, glowing with an unassuming light.

With a shaking hand, you activate the plugin. The cat meows, its emerald eyes glowing for a moment. It brushes against your leg again, purring loudly. "Greetings, player," a warm voice fills your ears, sounding both cat-like and strangely familiar. The cat grins, "Think of me as your ball of yarn. You know, like the one that helped a certain hero find his way out of a tricky maze ages ago. I'll help you through the tangled mess of Software Development City." The cat winks, "And who knows, we might even find some tasty treats along the way!" The text on the screen scrolls before your eyes. It's… this book. The cat is actually the book you're holding in your real-world hands, now transformed into a guide within the game.

"Software Development City might be broken," the Quest Helper continues, "but it's not unbeatable. Together, we'll find your way." The white cat turns and begins to stroll, his tail twitching invitingly. It's a familiar sight – a player-led companion you've seen in countless fantasy RPGs[2]. However, here in this crumbling city, he feels like a beacon of hope.

This fluffy Quest Helper might not be a guaranteed solution, but he is a weapon in this unfair game. You take a breath, steeling yourself. There's a better way. Time to break the vicious cycle of having experience without having a job. You'll learn by doing, building real things people use, networking with other developers, and finding ways to showcase your skills on an excellent resume. This will be your weapon against the rigged system. It might not be glamorous, but it'll get your foot in the door. And while you're grinding away at these real projects, you'll learn the skills companies need. You'll become a self-made developer, battle-tested and ready to beat this rigged game. Success won't come quickly, but you can master its rules and play to win. Time to see what fluffy can do.

---

[2] https://en.wikipedia.org/wiki/Role-playing_game

THE NEON ILLUSION

A s you depart Recruitment Outpost and the translucent white cat, your guide, melts away into the bustling heart of Software Development City, uncertainty creeps in. Success stories flicker above like digital motivational posters nobody really buys into. *"I taught myself to code in 3 months and landed a $150k job!"* The words flash, mocking. Another ad for a bootcamp promising quick fixes blares into view, and you can't help but let out a bitter laugh. The skyscrapers shimmer, but skepticism replaces awe. Success stories from those who've "made it" are everywhere, neon signs blaring, *"I did this, you can too!"* But beneath the glitter, doubts linger. The white cat promised to show you how to beat the system, but can he be that straightforward? Are these success stories genuinely attainable, or are they just illusions meant to lure you deeper into the maze?

A shadowy figure steps out of a nearby alleyway. "Rough day?" a voice calls out with a hint of amusement. You turn to see a man leaning casually against a lamppost, his worn leather jacket creaking as he shifts. He looks like he's seen everything this city can throw at someone.

"Thought so," he continues, nodding towards your clenched fist and the crumpled rejection letter peeking out of your pocket.

"The job board's a cruel mistress, isn't it? Keeps whispering sweet promises, then laughs as you chase the dragon." His smile widens, a touch of warmth seeping through the cynicism. "Good thing my little plugin is here to help," he says with a grin, and the white cat suddenly appears on his shoulder, purring softly.

"The name's Dan, by the way," he adds, extending a calloused hand. "I've been navigating these streets for a while now. Let's just say I've learned a few tricks that might just help you out."

As he speaks, a scruffy white cat magically appears on his shoulder, its emerald eyes scanning the surroundings. Dan nods toward the glowing ads above. "Those neon signs... tempting, right? The quick-win promise, the 'follow-my-blueprint' success story... But this city doesn't play by those rules." He scratches the cat's ear. "This little guy? He won't give you magic, but he can help you see through the BS."

Dan scoffs, gesturing toward the job quests that ask for impossible qualifications. "Those quests asking you to build the freakin' Matrix?" He shakes his head in disbelief. "Designed for one thing: keep you grinding, doubting yourself, right back on that next overpriced course." You listen intently as Dan unravels his own story: the theory-heavy university degree, the internships that went nowhere. It's not the perfect rise you expected, but it's... real, in a way the success stories never were.

His grin widens. "But then, I stumbled across those back alleys, the world of open source. Think of them like... like those rusty rental scooters you see in tourist traps. They're not glamorous; hell, some barely have wheels left. But get a few bolts tightened, figure out how the motor runs... those things will take you further than any packaged tour."

Dan explains how open-source projects are like unfinished products, released to the public for anyone to contribute to. You won't get paid instantly, but you'll build and experience the quests at the Recruitment Outpost demand. It's teamwork, learning how real-world products are built. He warns that not all projects succeed, but even failure teaches you what employers seek.

"Here's the thing," Dan emphasizes. "This white cat can't teach you how to write perfect code, but he can show you where to find these scooters to contribute with zero experience to start learning by doing. Imagine contributing to a real project used by real people. That's way more valuable than a fancy portfolio website you toiled over alone in your basement."

A mix of fear and excitement washes over you. Open source sounds messy and unpredictable. But there's a thrill to it, a sense that this isn't some prepared tutorial but the natural, gritty heart of the city.

"This isn't about choosing the perfect language," Dan warns. "It's about stopping chasing that perfect path and learning to ride the chaos. Because in that chaos... that's where you find the experience that the Recruitment Outpost keeps demanding."

"Think of it like this," he says, his voice a low rumble. "The University, the bootcamps, and online courses are like guided tours. They show you the sights, but do they really teach you to navigate on your own? To thrive in Software Development City, you need your own wheels."

A rumble cuts through the air as you're about to ask a question. A fleet of sleek silver scooters streaks past, heading out of the city and into a district marked *"Production Environments."* Developers you don't recognize, a determined look in their eyes, hold on tight. With a wave and a shout, "Hey! Ever seen anything like this before?" Dan yells, his voice raised to be heard over the whir of the electric engines. "This is the road of open source!" With a final grin and a wink, Dan reaches to pet the white cat, which suddenly bites him on the hand, causing him to grimace in pain. The cat jumps down from his shoulder and joins you, leaving Dan to disappear in a blur of motion, leaving you on the sidewalk as the electric hum of the scooters fades into the distance.

The cat's ears flattened in annoyance, a low growl rumbling in his throat as he stared at the spot where Dan had been standing. His tail twitched angrily. He hissed, "Hsss... Finally, that human left."

Calm returning, the cat turned his attention to you. His ears perked up, and his eyes widened with curiosity. He meowed softly, almost questioningly. "Ready to ditch the kiddie bike with training wheels, friend?"

He began to pace around you, his eyes never leaving your face. "It's time to decide," the cat said, voice low and challenging. "Coast along the pre-paved path or risk some scrapes to learn how to build roads no one's ever seen before."

Circling your feet, his tail still high, the cat continued, "Because out there, it's not textbooks that get you noticed." He looked up at you with pleading eyes. "The sweat stains on your code and the scars prove you went the extra mile."

The cat sat down, tail wrapped around his body, staring at you expectantly. With a mischievous glint in his eye, he added, "So, ready to claw your way to the top? Or do you need a nap first?"

SCENERY OF THE CITY

S o... did the challenge land? The world of open source offers both uncertainty and the exciting opportunity to build something real that can change the world. Like electric scooters, open-source software has the potential to revolutionize our processes with innovative solutions. Why do you need this book to understand the concept? We'll address this essential question in the upcoming chapters. Let's explore Software Development City together, where we'll encounter struggling newbies, helpful mentors, and moments of realization that this city can be shaped by you.

The white cat, your Quest Helper, appears beside you, tail twitching with excitement. He leaps onto your shoulder, nuzzling your neck. Suddenly, you find yourself lifting off the ground, the cityscape unfolding below you as you fly, guided by the cat. The sensation is exhilarating as you soar above the buildings, the wind rushing past.

You land softly in a quiet alley, sunlight dappling through the trees, casting shadows across a bewildering array of electric scooters. Each is different – some sleek and futuristic, others cobbled with mismatched parts. They buzz and whir, their LED displays flashing cryptic information that makes your head spin. You run a shaky hand through your hair. This was supposed to be the easy part, wasn't it? Choose your open-source project – your scooter, and hit the gas. But this overwhelming choice feels less like freedom and more like paralysis.

Now sitting calmly beside you, the white cat twitches his whiskers and purrs, "Lost in the scooter jungle, are we?"

You nod, relief mixing with a hint of frustration. "Exactly! How am I supposed to choose the right one? What if I make a mistake and end up with a lemon?"

The cat sprawls languidly, his eyes narrowing playfully. "That's the beauty of it, isn't it? There's no 'one size fits all' scooter here. Don't worry. Even the mightiest felines start as kittens."

You glance around, eyes darting from one scooter to the next, each model a potential path yet to be taken. Your mind races with possibilities and pitfalls. "But how do I even know what kind of ride I want?" you ask, gesturing helplessly at the rows of scooters.

The cat leaps onto a scooter, tail flicking. "Think of it as a test drive. No need to commit right away. Try a few and see what feels right. Don't worry, I'll help you understand it. We'll cover battery life, top speed, and those regenerative brakes you were concerned about."

A flicker of doubt creeps into your mind, the weight of indecision pressing down. "This all sounds great," you say hesitantly, "but what if choosing the right scooter takes forever? I mean, I've got bills to pay and a life to live. Can I really spend all my time tinkering around with these things?"

The alley fades, replaced by Software Development City's vibrant expanse. The cat nudges you, his soft purr vibrating through you. "Let's find out," he confidently says. With a flick of his tail, you both soar into the sky, the city sprawling beneath you. The wind whistles past as you fly, revealing a maze of potential below: bustling streets, towering skyscrapers, and hidden alleyways, each corner a new mystery waiting to be discovered.

The cat looks at you, his eyes sparkling. "Curiosity didn't kill the cat – it built the future. Ready for the ride of your life?"

WORK-LIFE BALANCE

Y ou and Quest Helper, the magical cat, land softly on a nearby rooftop of a quieter residential street, observing the scene below. A figure emerges from a sunlit apartment, backpack slung over one shoulder, briefcase in hand. He carefully lowers a sleek electric scooter from his porch steps, a familiar furrow between his brows.

The scooter's low hum sputters and dies. The man sighs, his shoulders slumping with a hint of defeat. "Just a minute, sweetie," he calls back through the open door, a hint of pleading in his voice. "Daddy's almost done getting you the smoothest ride in town."

The little girl's face appears in the doorway, eyes wide with a mix of anticipation and understanding. "Okay, Daddy," she replies, her voice barely a whisper. "But hurry, the swings are waiting!"

He smiles, a wave of love washing over his exhaustion. "I will, sweetheart." He crouches next to the scooter, his fingers moving with practiced ease. With a few clicks and adjustments of a loose wire, he fixes a nagging problem that had been causing the scooter to sputter all morning.

Snapping the tool compartment shut, he grabs her green helmet with dinosaurs and kneels to her eye level. "Alright, let's go, champ!" he says gently. "Helmet time first, though." He holds the helmet out, and she reaches up, looking at her daddy with wide eyes, waiting for the helmet. A smile spreads across his face. "Ready for adventure, huh?" He puts the helmet on her head and adjusts the straps. "There you go, good girl. Now let's show those swings who's boss!" He lifts her up and places her securely on the wide platform of the electric scooter, her laughter ringing out as they slowly and carefully take off down the street.

From your vantage point on the rooftop, you and Quest Helper, your magical cat companion, observe the scene below. Quest Helper stretches languidly, his tail flicking with curiosity. "Quite the touching scene, isn't it?" he purrs, his whiskers twitching.

You nod, still absorbing the father-daughter moment. Quest Helper leaps onto your shoulder, his fur brushing against your cheek. "Time to see more of Software Development City," he says, his voice carrying a hint of excitement. "Hold on tight."

Quest Helper takes flight with a graceful leap, and you follow, soaring through the warm midday air. The city's lights blur beneath you as you glide effortlessly, the sun high in the sky.

COMMUNITY WELCOMING

Y ou descend gracefully, landing on a quiet road near a brightly lit garage. Through the grime-streaked windows, you can see a kaleidoscope of scooters: vintage models with duct tape holding their side mirrors on, sleek new rides with glowing LED lights, and even a few cobbled-together contraptions that look like they were salvaged from a junkyard. Laughter spills onto the street, a cheerful counterpoint to the usual symphony of keyboard clicks and frustrated sighs.

You hesitate, a knot of anxiety tightening in your chest. Do you belong here? What if you're not good enough? The familiar imposter syndrome creeps in, whispering doubts in your ear. "Maybe I should just try this on my own," you mutter, looking down.

Sitting beside you, Quest Helper gives a playful swat at your shoe. "Nonsense," he says, his eyes twinkling with amusement. "Open source isn't a solo flight. It's about soaring together. Besides, who wants to fly alone when you can have fun with friends?" He grins, his whiskers twitching.

"But I'm afraid," you admit. "What if I can't keep up with them?"

The cat stretches lazily, his movements graceful and natural. "Trust me," he says, "connecting with other developers will only make your journey more enjoyable and rewarding. Plus, think of all the new tricks you can learn!" He flicks his tail playfully. "And if anyone gives you a hard time, I'll be here to purr-suade them otherwise." He winks, clearly enjoying his pun.

Before you can respond, a figure emerges from the garage. Her hair is a riot of purple, and her jumpsuit is covered in grease stains. A pair of welding goggles rests atop her head, and her smile is infectious. "Hey there, newbie!" she calls out. "You look a little lost. Come on in and meet the gang!"

You glance at Quest Helper, who nods encouragingly. With a deep breath, you follow her inside. The noise hits you like a wave: enthusiastic discussions about the latest software libraries, excited shouts about a new project launch and even a heated debate over the best way to brew coffee for all-nighters. It's chaotic, overwhelming... and undeniably welcoming.

The purple-haired dev pulls you towards a group huddled around a rusty scooter. "Check it out! I've been working on this for weeks," she says with pride. "I've made so many mistakes along the way, but that's how I've learned. Don't be afraid to mess up; it's part of the process." She laughs, "And now it finally purrs like a kitten." Quest Helper's ears perk up, and he quips, "A kitten, you say? Well, let's hope it doesn't come with claws!" The group laughs, and someone else chimes in, pointing out a potential modification for better battery life, sparking a passionate discussion.

"This is open source at its best," Quest Helper whispers, his voice cutting through the buzz. "Forget the stereotypes of lone geniuses and cutthroat competition. It's about shared passion and learning from one another. No one expects you to show up with a souped-up model. It's about what you contribute to the journey."

As the night unfolds, you join conversations, ask questions, and offer tentative suggestions. People listen, offer encouragement, and even laugh good-naturedly at your beginner mistakes. It's far from the cold, faceless competition you've experienced on job boards.

Quest Helper perches on a nearby workbench, observing the scene with satisfaction. "See?" he says, his voice warm and reassuring. "You're not alone. Every seasoned developer was once a beginner. Embrace the challenges and learn from those around you."

As the group disperses, you smile for the first time in a long while. Maybe, just maybe, this is where you belong. A flicker of excitement replaces the anxiety, a sense that you've found a place where it's okay to be a newbie, where collaboration is valued over competition, and where your voice matters.

Amidst the euphoria of finding a like-minded community in the open-source space, a nagging doubt begins to creep into your mind. While the collaborative spirit and sense of purpose are undeniable, you wonder how applicable these experiences will be when it comes to your job search. Will potential employers recognize the value of your contributions to open-source projects? Or will the unconventional nature of your work be a hindrance in a more traditional corporate setting?

As your mind churns with uncertainty, Quest Helper's eyes narrow, sensing your doubt. He stretches his paws and settles on your shoulder with a comforting weight.

"I can see you're not convinced," he murmurs, tail flicking thoughtfully. "Come with me. There's something you need to see – something that might change your mind about how employers view experience."

Before you can respond, a gust of wind lifts you both into the sky, sweeping you over the city as its lights pulse below like scattered stars.

THE PORTFOLIO UNVEILING

As you and the Quest Helper cat soar through the skies of Software Development City, the vibrant tapestry of the metropolis unfurls beneath you. The wind whispers past your ears, and the cityscape rushes in a blur of light and motion. The cat's fur glows softly in the twilight, adding a touch of magic to the journey.

"Hold on tight," Quest Helper purrs, a playful glint in his eye. "We're about to land."

You descend gracefully, landing on a ledge outside a tall, glass-paneled building. You peer through a window, observing a scene within. The cat nimbly hops onto the windowsill, his tail flicking with curiosity.

Inside, the hum of a corporate office fills the air. You see a young woman sitting, her hands fidgeting nervously. Her eyes dart around the room, revealing a sense of unease. Her gaze finally settles on the HR manager across the polished mahogany table.

The HR manager, a man with slicked-back hair and beady eyes, sneers. "Junior developer, is it?" he drawls, his voice dripping with condescension. "Let me tell you something, sweetheart. In this industry, experience is king. We need developers who can deliver results and add value to our company from day one."

The woman opens her mouth to speak, but the HR manager cuts her off with a dismissive wave of his hand. "Hold on there," he interrupts. "Let me guess – you built a personal website or maybe a simple app? Look, those are fine for beginners, but they don't demonstrate the kind of collaborative problem-solving skills we're looking for. We need developers who can hit the ground running on complex projects and integrate seamlessly into existing codebases. Can you tell me about any collaborative projects you've contributed to?"

Perched comfortably on the sill, Quest Helper leans in closer, his whiskers twitching with interest. "Watch closely," he whispers, a hint of amusement in his voice. "This is where it gets interesting."

The woman takes a deep breath, her voice unwavering as she replies, "I understand your concerns, sir. While I may not have traditional work experience, I've been actively involved in the open-source community." With a practiced gesture, she opens her laptop and projects her open-source profile onto the screen.

Lines of code flash before your eyes, a symphony of Python and JavaScript. The woman's voice, now confident and assured, guides them through the labyrinth of her projects. "Here's a chat app I built for a local community center," she explains, her fingers dancing across the touchpad. "It uses a real-time database and allows for seamless member communication."

The HR manager's skepticism softens into grudging interest. He leans forward, peppering the developer with questions about her contributions, the challenges faced, and the impact of her work. You see her eyes light up as she speaks; the love for her craft shines through.

Quest Helper's voice whispers in your ear, "This is more than just a job interview. It's a testament to the power of open-source contributions. This developer didn't spend years in a classroom;

she built her portfolio in the real world, contributing to projects that matter."

The HR manager's initial sneer slowly melts away as the presentation progresses. He grudgingly admits, "This is... surprisingly impressive. You seem to have a grasp of practical application that goes beyond what I expected."

The tension in the room dissipates, replaced by a palpable sense of relief. The developer's shoulders relax, and a radiant smile spreads across her face. She's done it. She's turned her passion into a career, not by following the well-trodden paths but by forging her own unique trail through the city of software development.

Quest Helper leaps down from the sill and pads over to you, his eyes sparkling with pride. "You see? A great portfolio is your golden ticket to Software Development City. It's not about credentials; it's about proving your worth through tangible contributions. Now, it's your turn to build your own masterpiece. Don't be afraid to experiment, to take risks, and let your passion guide you. The world is waiting to see what you can create."

As you both prepare to take flight, the city lights twinkle in the distance, calling you to explore its hidden corners and uncover your path to success. Feelings of excitement and expectation grow inside you, a hunger to create, contribute, and make your mark on this vibrant, ever-growing world of software development. With a shared chuckle, you and the magical cat launch into the air, ready to embrace the adventures that await in Software Development City.

OVERCOMING FEAR

You and Quest Helper glide into the darkness, the cool night air rushing past. The road ahead is pitch black, a mirror of the uncertainties before you. Your grip tightens on the handlebars as doubt creeps in. Without proper lighting, every turn, every bump, is a mystery. The path is hidden, and you wonder if you're truly ready for this journey.

"Maybe this is too hard," you think, the doubts from the job interview and your previous experiences surfacing again. "Am I even cut out for this? What if I choose the wrong direction and end up crashing?" The thought echoes your fears in real life – of making the wrong career move or life choice.

Just as you start to feel overwhelmed, Quest Helper begins to glow, casting a gentle, reassuring light around you. "No need to worry about the dark," he says with a soft chuckle, his eyes twinkling. "I'm your lighthouse tonight. Follow my light, and you'll stay on course."

You try to console yourself, thinking of this journey through Software Development City as a grand computer game. This abstraction helps distance your real-life stakes from the learning process, making setbacks feel less personal and more like game challenges. In a game, the worst that can happen is losing a life or restarting a level. Each attempt teaches you to navigate obstacles more effectively. Hitting a dead end isn't the end; it's merely a pause to reflect on how far you've come. When you create your resume, it will be like saving your game progress, showcasing your resilience, learning curve, and real-world achievements. This record of progress will be your ticket to completing the main quest of landing your first job in the tech industry.

You glance down at the glowing cat, his soft fur shimmering like starlight. "Thanks, Quest Helper," you say, feeling gratitude. "I was afraid of going alone, but it feels less daunting with you here."

Quest Helper flicks his tail, his eyes sparkling with amusement. "Of course! Besides, what kind of magical guide would I be if I let you wander aimlessly in the dark? Now, keep your eyes on the road and trust the journey."

As Quest Helper lights the way, you begin to see the outlines of dozens of electric scooters parked along the roadside. Each scooter's sleek lines and flashing lights beckon, each a different model, a distinct promise. Your earlier doubts dissipate, replaced by a growing curiosity and excitement.

Quest Helper purrs reassuringly. "Remember, every great journey starts with a single step – or, in our case, a single ride. It's not about the perfect start; it's about starting. Trust the process and take it one step at a time."

With the cat's light guiding you, the darkness loses its menace. You're not alone. Quest Helper's presence and encouragement transform your fear into determination. You mount a sleek scooter, feeling the engine's hum beneath you.

As you ride through the night, the city reveals its secrets. The darkness becomes a canvas waiting to be explored. Each turn, each path, brings discovery and progress. You smile, confidence and excitement surging within you. With Quest Helper by your side, you're no longer afraid. The journey is long, but you're ready to face whatever challenges come your way.

As dawn breaks, the first light of a new day mirrors the start of your new career in software development. The horizon glows with promise, and you ride towards it, ready to beat this game.

PART II
From Passenger to Pilot

WELCOME TO THE SCOOTER SPOT

I magine GitHub[3] as the central hub of the world of open source, where each scooter represents a unique project waiting for new contributors. GitHub isn't just a hosting service; it's a vibrant community space where developers from all backgrounds come together to build, share, and improve software. Here, you'll find projects of all kinds, from beginner-friendly ones to challenging, high-speed initiatives. By selecting a project on GitHub, you're not simply choosing a mode of transportation – you're joining a team journey, contributing to a shared ecosystem where each update and improvement has a real impact.

Before diving into the world of open source, let's explore some essential tools and ideas. Open-source software is like the scooter you're about to ride: it's accessible, flexible, and driven by the community. The source code is openly shared, allowing anyone to inspect, improve, or adapt it, fostering collaboration and continuous enhancement. Just as scooters make transportation accessible to everyone in a city, open-source software makes

---

[3] https://github.com/

technology more accessible and adaptable for everyone in the digital world.

The foundation of open source is built on shared contributions and global collaboration. With developers around the world adding to and maintaining these projects, open-source software is constantly improving, secure, and openly available to all. Each new contributor strengthens the foundation – like a network of roads that become more connected and reliable as more people contribute.

As you start working on an open-source project, you'll experience this unique world of collaborative development. It's like joining a traffic flow on your chosen scooter: you'll navigate alongside other developers, each contributing to the project's forward momentum. You'll learn from experienced developers, add your unique perspective, and advance the project together. Working together is essential in open source, much like weaving through traffic with skill and cooperation.

So, are you ready to embark on this journey? Picture downloading a scooter app for developers – your gateway to exploring open source. To get started, visit GitHub's sign-up page[4]. Here, you'll create your account, securing your space within the community. Enter your email, create a password, and choose a username. This becomes your identifier, allowing others to recognize your contributions and collaborations.

After signing up, check your email for verification, complete the puzzle, and you're ready to go! Welcome to GitHub – where your open-source adventure begins. Here, you'll connect, share, and grow, joining a vibrant community that builds the future together.

---

[4] https://github.com/signup

TRAFFIC LIGHT METHOD

N avigating the vast world of software development can feel overwhelming. But like entering a bustling city for the first time, the adventure takes shape as you learn to explore it step by step. Each project is a path forward – some more accessible to start with, others offering challenges that push you further. Your mission is to discover the project that sparks your interest and aligns with your growth as a developer.

We introduce the Traffic Light Method to help you navigate this journey (Figure 1). This structured, four-step approach provides a practical roadmap for finding and contributing to open-source projects with clarity and purpose. Imagine yourself at a crossroads, surrounded by traffic lights. This is where the traffic light method comes into play, transforming each light into a milestone on your journey.

STEP 1: WHAT THE WORLD NEEDS

Are you feeling trapped or annoyed by the current situation? That's excellent. It marks an ideal starting point. This is your red light – the moment when you might feel unsure about your next steps. Begin by becoming an observer of the world's challenges. Look for problems that spark your interest – gaps in healthcare access, educational barriers, environmental concerns, or community disconnection. The key is finding issues that both matter to society and resonate with you personally. This initial phase isn't about having solutions; it's about discovery. Each global challenge represents a potential quest line where your future contributions could turn the tide.

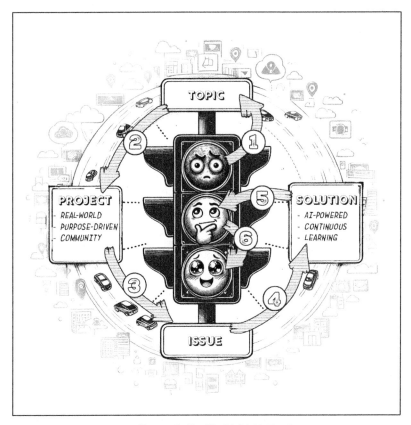

Figure 1: Traffic Light Method

STEP 2: CHOOSING YOUR PROJECT

With your world map marked with potential quests, the next step is to choose an open-source project that resonates with your goals. This is where you connect with a community working on something specific, allowing you to find a sense of purpose and direction. By selecting a project, you'll start to see where your skills fit and what you can contribute, giving you an idea of your specialization. Whether front end, back end, or something else entirely, your role will take shape as you dive deeper into the project.

STEP 3: SELECTING YOUR TASK

Once you've chosen your project, it's time to narrow your focus by selecting a specific task or issue to tackle. This is your opportunity to make an impact while sharpening your skills. Tasks can range from fixing a bug to developing new features, depending on your experience and interests. Taking on a well-defined task gives you a clear starting point and allows you to work toward solving a real-world problem step by step.

STEP 4: SOLVING THE TASK AND GROWING

This is where the real work begins, and your journey to growth takes off. It's about learning the basics like coding, debugging, and problem-solving while sharpening skills like critical thinking and communication. With AI tools as your co-pilot, you can streamline learning, automate repetitive tasks, and focus on creative problem-solving. The yellow light represents the process of working on the task, where steady effort and learning guide you forward. The green light signifies the moment of success when you solve the task and are ready to move on to your next challenge. Each green light is a milestone, showing how far you've come and preparing you for the next step in your journey. By embracing this cycle, you'll continuously grow, gain confidence, and make meaningful contributions to your project and the world.

$$\Delta\Delta\Delta$$

At this point, it's perfectly okay to feel overwhelmed. The path ahead might seem like an endless mountain to climb, and you may be tempted to close this book and set it aside. "It's too much," you might think, looking at these four steps stretching before you. Those feelings of doubt and uncertainty? They're not just valid – they're part of the journey.

But here's a truth worth holding onto: if you stick with it, keep this book close, and eventually land a job inspired by these principles, you'll look back at this moment with gratitude. Every successful developer has stood where you're standing now, feeling that same mix of anticipation and uncertainty.

In the chapters ahead, we'll dive deep into that crucial first step: identifying what the world needs and how you can make your mark through open-source contributions. We'll explore the landscape of problems waiting to be solved, discover where to find promising projects and learn how to match your growing skills with real-world needs. Every question you have about finding your place in the open-source community – we'll address it.

For now, though, focus on taking just one step forward. That's all you need to do. Chapter by chapter, concept by concept, we'll build your path to success together. As the saying goes, *"It always seems impossible until it's done."*

STEP 1
Topic

THE IMPORTANCE OF PURPOSE

The classic advice, *"Do what you love, and you'll never work another day in your life,"* sounds like a perfect cheat code for career happiness. But in the real world of software development, passion is just one component of a more complex algorithm.

Before writing your first line of code or choosing a programming language, it's crucial to consider a foundational question: What is your reason for being? This question acts like a compass, guiding you not just toward a job but toward a career that aligns with your deeper values and goals.

You might wonder, "Why start with such an abstract question? I'm here to learn software development and secure a stable career." It's a valid thought. But approaching your career without understanding your larger goals is like setting out on a long road trip without a map. You may cover distance but risk ending up in places you never intended to go (Screenshot 1).

Think of yourself as a character in an open-world game who's just spawned in this bustling metropolis of software development. At first, you might be content to follow the tutorial prompts, learn basic commands, and collect achievements. But as you progress, you'll need to choose your path carefully. Your sense of purpose becomes the full beam that lights up the path through the dense fog of choices and challenges. Each line of code becomes a step in your journey, and each project is a new district to explore.

r/django · 8 mo. ago

_Broken_Coder_

WTF is happening with me

Hello everyone I will make it short, I love web dev since high school but the problem is i was changing my mind a lot, my roadmap was not clear some times learn cyber security then go back to web dev and bounce between web technologies a lot, And go through tutorial hell, I have realized my mistakes but after wasting 4 years of my life, now i am 25 years old unemployed and i have financial problems, through this journey i learned Python and Django i am welling to stick with it but i feel that i have no power anymore to do anything.

Screenshot 1: A Reddit user is unhappy with his career path in tech.
https://www.reddit.com/r/django/comments/1dfchfj/

The quest for a meaningful life is universal. Sooner or later, everyone faces this challenge. As you level up in this vast digital city, you'll discover that this journey can become more than a way to earn money – it can grow into something that truly excites you. Financial incentives can motivate, but they often lead to quick burnout, leaving you feeling adrift.

While technical skills can be taught and jobs secured, they don't guarantee long-term satisfaction. Imagine waking up to a career that feels like an endless loop – monotonous tasks that leave you stuck in the grind. It's like being in a video game where you've mastered the level but are forced to replay the same daily quests over and over. Purpose ensures that every project you undertake and every skill you acquire contributes to something greater.

Purpose isn't just about lofty ideals; it's about creating clarity. Knowing why you're doing what you do builds resilience, helps you navigate challenges, and provides motivation when the journey gets tough. Whether debugging a complex system or developing solutions for a startup, aligning your work with what truly matters to you transforms it from a routine task into a meaningful pursuit.

Finding your purpose can be challenging, especially when uncertain about what excites you or where your strengths lie. Purpose isn't always something you find instantly; sometimes, it's something you build step by step. The first step is often the hardest but also the most crucial.

In the next chapter, we'll explore practical ways to uncover what drives you and connect it with opportunities like those you can discover on GitHub. We'll discuss where to seek inspiration, how to seek guidance, and what to do if nothing immediately sparks your interest. This is your starting point, and every step forward brings you closer to discovering a career that truly aligns with who you are.

A SEA OF POSSIBILITIES

Y ou know you want to make a lasting impact on the world, but choosing the right topic can be daunting. With the vast digital landscape at your fingertips, you stand at a crossroads, wondering where your contributions could be most meaningful.

The digital world, particularly GitHub, is a treasure trove of projects spanning countless topics. For you, this represents a sea of opportunities, each beckoning with the promise of making a difference.

Healthcare and social good projects can be incredibly impactful, aiming to improve lives and communities. Open-source initiatives in this domain offer the chance to develop and share tools that address pressing health challenges, from tracking disease outbreaks to providing telemedicine services in underserved areas. By contributing to these projects, you can leverage your coding skills to create solutions that improve patient outcomes, streamline healthcare delivery, and promote overall well-being. If you share this vision of using technology as a force for good, you can collaborate with a global community dedicated to making a tangible difference in people's lives.

Sustainability and climate change initiatives are crucial areas of focus. By engaging with these projects, you align yourself with a global effort to address environmental challenges and promote a sustainable future. Your involvement may include contributing to climate modeling tools, developing software for renewable energy, or supporting platforms that advance environmental awareness. Every contribution adds to a collective effort to reduce the effects of climate change and foster ecological stewardship. Embracing these opportunities allows you to use your skills for a purpose beyond immediate technical achievements, ensuring that your work contributes to a meaningful and lasting positive impact on the world.

Education projects offer another avenue for impact. Contributing to open-source educational tools and platforms can help democratize access to knowledge, breaking down barriers for learners everywhere. These projects often involve developing learning management systems, creating interactive educational content, and building platforms that facilitate remote learning and collaboration. Your contributions can empower educators and students, providing them with the necessary resources to succeed in an increasingly digital world. This work fosters individual growth and promotes lifelong learning and intellectual curiosity globally.

Community-driven governance and decentralized autonomous organizations (DAOs) represent a new frontier. These open-source projects intrigue you with their potential to reshape societal structures and empower communities. By participating in the development of DAOs, you can contribute to creating transparent, decentralized decision-making systems that give individuals a greater voice in the governance of their communities. These projects explore innovative ways to organize, collaborate, and distribute resources, offering a glimpse into a future where power is more evenly distributed, and collective action is facilitated by technology.

Artificial intelligence projects stand at the intersection of technological innovation and groundbreaking discovery. You are drawn to the idea of contributing to open-source AI initiatives that push the boundaries of what's possible. These projects range from developing machine learning algorithms that can predict and analyze complex systems to creating AI-driven tools that revolutionize industries like healthcare, scientific research, and technological infrastructure. By working on open-source AI projects, you can help drive technological advancement, focusing on cutting-edge algorithms, innovative problem-solving, and the transformative potential of artificial intelligence to reshape our understanding of computation and intelligence.

Amidst this expansive digital realm, the game development and gamification world stands out with its profound potential to transform experiences and influence society. Creating engaging, immersive games entertains, educates, inspires, and brings people together. By developing games that address real-world issues or promote positive behaviors, you can harness the power of interactive storytelling to effect meaningful change. The gamification of various aspects of life, from education to fitness, opens up new avenues to motivate and engage people in ways that traditional methods cannot. This exciting field invites you to blend creativity with technology, crafting experiences that captivate, contribute to a better world, or just create games for fun.

Selecting the global challenge in the continuously evolving realm of software development can be daunting. But don't worry; you're not alone in this journey. Imagine having a wise and knowledgeable companion by your side, an AI chatbot designed to guide you through the complexities of your interests and skills. This digital ally is more than just an algorithm; it's a beacon of insight, ready to help you navigate the intricacies of software development and make decisions that align with your passions and talents.

As we start this journey, your AI companion will be your helpful partner, offering advice, support, and useful tips along the way. It's more than just a tool – it's like a friend who's here to guide you through the exciting world of software development. With your AI companion by your side, the journey will feel less overwhelming and much more exciting.

In the next chapter, we'll talk about how your AI companion can help you find your purpose. It will make things clearer, help you focus, and even show you new possibilities you might not have thought about. Together, you'll explore the big world of technology and discover where you fit in. With its help and your determination, there's no limit to what you can achieve.

FROM SIDEKICKS TO SAGES

R emember the companions from your favorite video games? They'd carry your extra loot when your inventory was overflowing. Though they might seem quirky with their occasional odd jokes, they are far more than simple sidekicks nowadays. Imagine these companions in the bustling city of software development – digital assistants who don't just carry your virtual gear but help you navigate complex technological landscapes.

As we enter the era of artificial intelligence, these digital companions have evolved from simple assistants to intelligent guides. They are sophisticated entities that offer insights and advice on various topics. This shift fundamentally changes our interactions with technology, making each digital encounter a learning opportunity. As you navigate Software Development City, these AI companions are ready to engage in conversations about anything.

Though I mention specific chatbots, the landscape changes so quickly that such details may soon become outdated. At the time of writing, pioneers like ChatGPT[5], Google Gemini[6], Microsoft Copilot[7], and Anthropic Claude[8] are leading the way in AI companion technology. For the most current updates, visit my website[9], where I strive to keep information fresh and relevant.

Each AI companion might seem similar at first glance, but spending time with them reveals their unique personalities and strengths. To begin your exploration, try initiating a conversation with a simple, purposeful prompt: *"Help me find an interesting topic on GitHub that could make a meaningful impact on global challenges."* Let the conversation flow. Let it be natural. Ask follow-up questions about topics you are particularly interested in, and the AI companion will provide further suggestions and insights.

Mastering prompt engineering is crucial for effective AI interactions. It involves crafting inputs that guide AI tools to generate accurate and useful outputs. Various resources can help you improve this skill, including OpenAI's guide[10], Microsoft's recommendations for Copilot prompts[11], Google Workspace's prompting tips[12], and Anthropic's overview of working with Claude[13]. Applying these principles can transform your interactions into productive collaborations, unlocking the potential of AI companions.

In the next chapter, I'll share my personal "true north" topic that transformed my journey, with the aim of inspiring you to discover your unique path in Software Development City, enhanced by AI's collaborative potential.

---

[5] https://chatgpt.com
[6] https://gemini.google.com
[7] https://copilot.microsoft.com
[8] https://claude.ai
[9] https://greenlightcareer.tech/book/sidekicks
[10] https://platform.openai.com/docs/guides/prompt-engineering
[11] https://copilot.cloud.microsoft/prompts
[12] https://support.google.com/a/users/answer/14200040
[13] https://docs.anthropic.com/en/docs/build-with-claude/
    prompt-engineering/overview

SPARK ON THE COUCH

T he glow of the television danced across my living room, re-flecting in my tired eyes as I scrolled aimlessly through the Netflix library. It was just another Thursday night, another post-work slump on the familiar comfort of my couch.

At 30, my life wasn't bad. It wasn't perfect, but it was comfortable. I had a decent apartment in a bustling tech city, a stable and well-paying job, and the best part – a wife and our giggling one-year-old daughter. The joy of fatherhood was still fresh, the sleepless nights a distant memory replaced by the wonder of watching our little girl explore the world.

Yet, amidst the comfort, a gnawing feeling lingered beneath the surface. It was a quiet discontent, a sense of something missing.

The mindless scrolling was abruptly interrupted by a documentary thumbnail titled Breaking Boundaries: The Science of Our Planet.[14] A wave of familiarity washed over me. Of course, I had heard about climate change and seen the news snippets and the warnings. But it had always existed on the periphery, a distant rumble overshadowed by the immediate concerns of daily life.

---

[14] https://www.netflix.com/title/81336476

With a click, the documentary began. As the opening scenes unfolded, showcasing the stark realities of our changing planet, a jolt of electricity ran through me. The information wasn't entirely new, but this time, it hit differently. The situation's urgency became crystal clear. I realized there is scientific consensus that the world is heading in the wrong direction. I don't understand why something scientifically proven becomes a political discourse. My "common sense" tells me if scientific research is so united in stating something like smoking is bad or that the Earth is round, why shouldn't we believe in human-made climate change? It's just common sense. I started feeling a strange mix of emotions – fear, anger, and a spark of something unexpected – hope.

This wasn't just someone else's problem anymore. It was a tangible threat, looming over the world in which we carelessly built a future. For the first time, I saw myself as part of the solution, not just a bystander.

The documentary ended, leaving a profound impact on me. I couldn't shake the feeling of urgency, the need to do something, anything. But what? I was a software developer skilled in coding and building digital solutions. What contribution could I make to a problem this vast, complex problem?

The answer, I realized, wasn't immediately clear. But one thing was sure – I couldn't stay on that couch, passively scrolling through life. There was a fire now ignited within me, a spark that refused to be extinguished. It was the spark of purpose, a determination to use my skills to fight for a better future, not just for myself and my family but for future generations, my daughter's generation.

I knew the journey ahead wouldn't be easy. It would require exploration, learning, and perhaps even a complete shift in perspective. But as I looked towards the future, the spark within me flickered brighter, fueled by a newfound sense of purpose and the unwavering belief that change, however small, was within reach.

Frustration gnawed at me. How could something so crucial to humanity's survival receive such a lukewarm response? People seemed content to stay in their comfortable bubbles, oblivious to the storm brewing on the horizon. Fueled by a newfound purpose, I launched myself into research, scouring the internet for any way to bridge this gap in awareness.

That's when I stumbled upon Climate Mind[15]. This non-profit open-source project aimed to simplify conversations about climate change, making complex science accessible to the everyday individual. Its innovative approach resonated deeply with my desire to make a difference.

Joining the project as a volunteer developer was like a homecoming. The sense of purpose I felt, collaborating with a team passionate about the same cause, was unlike anything I had experienced before. This, not the comfortable routine of my day job, brought true fulfillment. It was a feeling of contributing to something bigger than myself, leaving a positive mark on the world.

Looking back, I realize that my newfound passion coincided with a significant shift in my personal narrative. The arrival of our daughter undoubtedly amplified my desire to leave behind a better world. It was as if fatherhood had unlocked a new level of commitment. This responsibility transcended the boundaries of self-preservation. Now, the future I envisioned wasn't just for myself but for this tiny, curious person who filled our lives with so much love and laughter.

But what if you don't feel that spark, that internal compass directing you towards a purpose? Don't despair. Sometimes, the path unfolds in unexpected ways, like a chance encounter with the love of your life.

If you haven't found your "true north" yet, that's perfectly alright. A good starting point can sometimes be a simple spark of interest, a captivating buzzword, or even a specific programming

---

[15] https://climatemind.org/

language. The next chapter will explore how these seemingly mundane interests can blossom into unexpected journeys, leading you closer to your unique purpose.

BEYOND THE RED LIGHT

D on't worry if you're not yet driven by a grand vision to change the world or if inspiration hasn't struck like lightning. That's perfectly fine. The spark you're looking for often emerges through action rather than anticipation. Starting your IT journey with the innovative traffic light method doesn't require a world-changing idea – just your willingness to take the first step.

Before picking up this book, you've likely encountered various discussions about roles and programming languages within the IT realm. Think of this knowledge as a window overlooking the vast and dynamic Software Development City, offering glimpses of the many roads you can explore.

You might be wondering what type of work truly excites you. Does the idea of crafting sleek website interfaces appeal to you? Or does building iPhone apps spark your curiosity? The beauty of this journey is that it's entirely customizable – tailored to your interests and goals. Picture yourself navigating the bustling streets of this metaphorical city, moving steadily toward your desired destination.

An AI chatbot, your trusted ally on this adventure, can help light the way. It can answer essential questions like which programming language is best for web development or what tools are crucial for venturing into data science. This dialogue bridges the gap between your curiosity and actionable steps.

At this early stage, your focus shouldn't be on mastering every detail but on finding a general direction that excites you. If the thought of choosing a programming language seems daunting, fear not. Think of your first steps in Software Development City as broad brushstrokes – playful, exploratory, and unpressured.

This book intentionally avoids naming specific languages because the tech world is ever-changing. Instead, your task is to leverage AI as your guide in this constantly shifting landscape. This isn't just about identifying the right tools; it's an opportunity to hone your research skills – a fundamental ability for any developer.

As you explore and build these skills, you'll soon find yourself moving beyond the red lights of the traffic light method. This isn't about racing to mastery but reaching a point where the red light no longer halts your progress. You're beginning to accelerate toward the green lights that symbolize the freedom to move confidently as an aspiring software developer.

With this momentum, you're now ready to embark on this exciting phase, steering your journey toward hands-on experience and real-world applications. Let's ride into the next chapter, where the adventure of project selection awaits, a crucial step in navigating the roads of your software development career.

STEP 2

Project

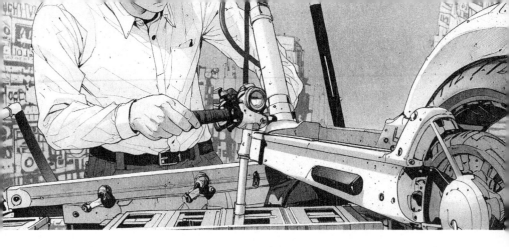

UNDER THE HOOD

A t that moment, as you stand before the sleek, matte black machine, doubt creeps into your mind. You question your decision to embark on this adventure, to leave the familiar behind and embrace the unknown. What exactly is this scooter?

This scooter represents your entry into the world of GitHub projects, also known as repositories. A repository is not just a digital folder; it's a universe of its own, brimming with ideas, codes, and the collective intellect of developers from around the globe. Like choosing a scooter for its agility and simplicity, selecting a GitHub project to contribute to is your first step towards an adventurous journey in coding.

Think of a repository as your scooter's structure – compact yet comprehensive. At its core, a repository is indeed a folder, but one that carries within it the DNA of a project: its code, documentation, and history. Each file, each line of code, is part of a larger story, much like every component of your scooter is vital for its smooth ride. This simplicity and structure make your journey through software development both manageable and exciting.

The maintainers serve as the guardians of each project, akin to the dedicated service team of your trusty scooter. These individuals or teams are the project's heartbeat, ensuring that every cog runs smoothly, every line of code serves its purpose, and the community thrives. They're not just caretakers; they're visionaries who chart the course of the project, responding to feature requests, managing bug reports, and fostering discussions. Engaging with them, you'll find guidance, mentorship, and the opportunity to contribute meaningfully to the project's journey. They are the ones who decide whether your contributions are aligned with the project's goals and standards, and they are the ones who ultimately merge your PRs into the project.

Every scooter comes with a manual created by maintainers, a guide that introduces you to its features, how to use it, and how to ensure a safe ride. In the world of GitHub, the manual's first page is the README.md file. It's the first thing you encounter when you visit a repository. This file acts as the project's introduction, offering a comprehensive overview of what the project is about, its purpose, and how to get involved. Other resources linked from a GitHub project can provide an understanding of the project. These materials often include links to the project's official website, exhaustive documentation, and other essential resources. These are your go-to for grasping the project's structure, interacting with its community, and making significant contributions.

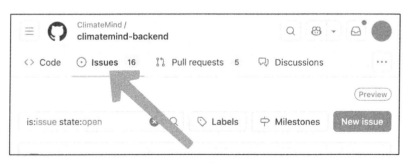

Screenshot 2: Issues tab in a GitHub project.
https://github.com/ClimateMind/climatemind-backend/issues

The GitHub Issues section (Screenshot 2) is a critical component of any project, acting as the primary hub for communication and collaboration among developers and users alike. This platform allows for the reporting of bugs, the requesting of new features, and the initiation of discussions on various aspects of the project. It's a space where the community comes together to share ideas, solve problems, and collectively improve the project. As a contributor, engaging with GitHub Issues allows you to understand the project's current challenges and areas of focus, providing valuable insights into how you can contribute meaningfully.

Pull Requests[16] (PRs) are the mechanism through which contributions are made to a project (Screenshot 3). Developers inform maintainers of changes by forking the repository, applying modifications, and submitting a PR. This PR details the changes, rationale, and context. Maintainers review it, initiating discussions, modification requests, or clarifications. Merged PRs indicate achievement, validate your work, and impact the project's evolution, making your contributions foundational.

Screenshot 3: GitHub project's Pull Requests section.
https://github.com/ClimateMind/climatemind-backend/pulls

Contributing to a GitHub project enhances its functionality and connects you with the community. This fosters a sense of accomplishment while offering valuable learning experiences in collaborative software development. As you progress, you'll find opportunities to enhance skills, grow your network, and influence open-source project's future. This mirrors commercial software development, making the skills you gain equally valuable.

---

[16] https://docs.github.com/en/pull-requests

MORE THAN STICKERS

Welcome back, intrepid explorer! We've arrived at a pivotal moment in our journey through the sprawling metropolis of software development, where you transition from a curious observer to an active participant.

Remember those compelling challenges we discussed earlier that ignited your sense of purpose? Now, it's time to fan that spark into a flame of passion as we explore the practical steps of choosing projects that align with your interests. As we've established, selecting projects that resonate with your passions is crucial. It ensures that each contribution not only hones your skills but also reflects your values and aspirations.

Let's talk about GitHub, our digital city's sprawling scooter hub. It features a unique feature called Topics, which acts like vibrant stickers on each scooter, each representing a specific area of software development. Whether you're passionate about machine learning, intrigued by web development, or eager to explore data science, GitHub Topics are your way to find projects that match your interests and ambitions.

Imagine you're passionate about environmental issues; you wouldn't want to ride a scooter adorned with racing stripes. Instead, you'd seek out one with a green leaf sticker, signaling projects focused on sustainability and eco-conscious technology. Similarly, GitHub Topics serve as signposts, guiding you to where your unique talents and passions can thrive.

These topics are more than just labels; they're gateways to communities of like-minded developers. By engaging with these communities, you'll access a wealth of knowledge, mentorship, and collaboration opportunities, allowing you to learn from seasoned developers, share insights, and contribute to projects with real-world impact.

Exploring GitHub's Topics[17] is like opening a treasure chest of the most popular subjects within the GitHub universe. This diverse array showcases everything from cutting-edge technologies to foundational software practices. Each topic leads to a new realm of possibilities, offering you a chance to learn, grow, and make an impact in the open-source community.

If navigating GitHub's vast array of Topics seems overwhelming, the search bar is your invaluable tool. Typing *topic:"climate-change"* into the search bar quickly finds projects dedicated to environmental sustainability[18].

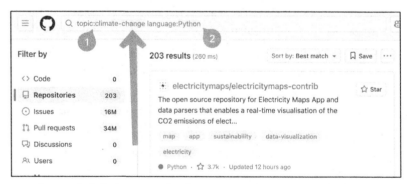

Screenshot 4: An example of a topic search using specific terms.
https://github.com/search?q=topic%3Aclimate-change
+language%3APython+&type=repositories

---

[17] https://github.com/topics
[18] https://github.com/search?q=topic%3A%22climate-change%22&type= repositories

Searching by programming language can further refine your search. Using a phrase like *language:"Python"* narrows down the vast project landscape to those coded in Python (Screenshot 4).

You can also directly navigate to topics by adding the topic name to the URL, such as https://github.com/topics/climate (Screenshot 5).

So, as you stand before this array of digital scooters, let your purpose and passion guide you. Seek out the topics that resonate with your heart and spark your curiosity. While the vastness of GitHub's Topics might initially seem daunting, there are curated Awesome Lists to streamline your exploration. These lists, which we'll explore in our next chapter, are like highlighted routes on your map, leading you to the most scenic and enriching paths. With your passions fueling you and these lists as your guide, the journey ahead promises to be exhilarating, refining your skills and contributing meaningfully to software development.

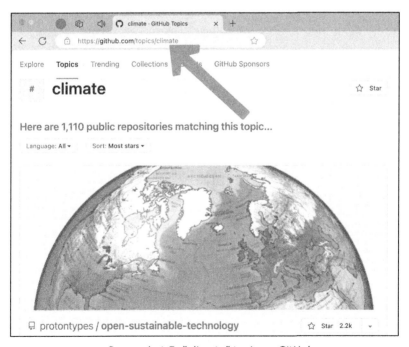

Screenshot 5: "climate" topic on GitHub.
https://github.com/topics/climate

AWESOME!

Y ou've just navigated through the vast expanse of GitHub
Topics. Still, the path to genuinely igniting your passion in
open source sometimes leads you down a less-trodden path. Think
of it this way: you've been looking for treasure by digging in the
most prominent spots, but what if the real gems are hidden in a
secret, winding path through an overgrown forest? Enter the Awesome Lists, the hidden treasure maps of the world of open source.

Head over to the Awesome topic[19] and prepare to be amazed.
These Awesome Lists aren't just another topic; they're the pulsating heart of the open-source community. Each list is a curated
treasure chest assembled by enthusiasts who've poured their passion and expertise into gathering the most valuable resources on
any subject. Imagine walking into a grand library where each shelf
is stocked with tomes of wisdom waiting for you to explore.

What makes these lists truly special is their dynamic nature.
They're living documents, constantly evolving with contributions
from the community. This is where the spirit of open-source
shines brightest; knowledge isn't just shared, it's expanded upon,
ensuring everyone benefits. Joining the world of Awesome Lists is

---

[19] https://github.com/topics/awesome

like becoming part of an explorer's guild, where each member adds their findings to a collective map that grows richer daily.

You can use a straightforward and effective GitHub strategy to pinpoint the resources you need for your chosen topic. By combining your topic of interest with the keyword *"awesome"* in your search query, like *topic:"climate-change" topic:"awesome"*, you will be directed to all the Awesome Lists related to your topic[20]. This method simplifies finding valuable and impactful projects to contribute to, especially in areas you're passionate about, such as climate change and sustainability.

When exploring topics like climate on GitHub, projects categorized under Awesome often appear at the top of the search results, reflecting their popularity and the value they offer to the community. One notable example is the Open Sustainable Technology repository[21]. This project is a primary resource for anyone looking to contribute to climate-related technology. It hosts a comprehensive list of open-source technologies focused on sustainability, making it an ideal starting point for contributions.

The GitHub repository Awesome Health[22] is an excellent resource for those interested in healthcare. It aggregates a wide range of open-source projects, tools, and libraries specifically focused on healthcare, offering a valuable starting point for contributions in this field.

Blockchain enthusiasts should explore the collection of DeFi & blockchain resources and tools DeFi Developer Road Map[23]. Additionally, the Awesome Blockchain repository[24] is another solid foundation for anyone looking into blockchain technology, providing a curated list of projects and resources.

---

[20] https://github.com/search?q=topic%3A%22climate-change%22
+topic%3A%22awesome%22&type=repositories
[21] https://github.com/protontypes/open-sustainable-technology
[22] https://github.com/kakoni/awesome-healthcare
[23] https://github.com/OffcierCia/DeFi-Developer-Road-Map
[24] https://github.com/yjjnls/awesome-blockchain

Beginners looking for an entry point into a specific technology can start with the Awesome List for Beginners[25]. This list is designed to help newcomers navigate the vast array of technologies by highlighting projects particularly welcoming to new contributors.

For those drawn to machine learning, the Awesome Machine Learning repository[26] compiles an impressive collection of machine-learning frameworks, libraries, and software. It's an invaluable resource for anyone looking to engage with the machine-learning community and contribute to its growth.

For those specifically interested in generative AI, the Awesome Generative AI collection[27] offers a curated list of generative AI projects, tools, and resources. This repository is an excellent starting point for anyone exploring the cutting-edge field of generative artificial intelligence.

For those with a passion for game development, GitHub offers a treasure trove of resources to explore. The GitHub Topics page dedicated to games[28] is an excellent starting point, showcasing various game-related projects, from full-fledged games to game engines and utilities.

Diving deeper into the world of game development, the Awesome Gamedev list[29] is a comprehensive collection of tools, engines, and resources for game creators. For those seeking a more magical touch in their game development endeavors, the Magic Tools repository[30] offers a delightful assortment of game development resources.

Suppose you're looking to contribute to or learn from existing open-source games. In that case, the Open-source Games repository[31] is a goldmine. This collection showcases a variety of open-

---

[25] https://github.com/MunGell/awesome-for-beginners
[26] https://github.com/josephmisiti/awesome-machine-learning
[27] https://github.com/steven2358/awesome-generative-ai
[28] https://github.com/topics/games
[29] https://github.com/Calinou/awesome-gamedev
[30] https://github.com/ellisonleao/magictools
[31] https://github.com/bobeff/open-source-games

source games across different genres and platforms. It's like wandering through a gallery of interactive art, where each game is playable and an opportunity to peek behind the curtain and understand the magic that makes it work.

These lists aren't just for browsing but serve as a springboard for your open-source journey. Each entry is a potential starting point, a spark that could ignite your curiosity and guide you toward a project that perfectly aligns with your purpose and areas of interest. Every exploration and discovery brings you closer to finding the right project that resonates with you in the world of software development.

And remember, encountering crossroads without signs is expected in your journey through the city of software development. If you find yourself at such a junction, unable to discern the direction towards projects that pique your interest, don't hesitate to turn to your AI companion for guidance. Consulting your AI whenever you face a blockade in your quest is a wise habit. This digital ally is equipped to illuminate paths you might not have noticed, offering insights and solutions regardless of the challenge at hand.

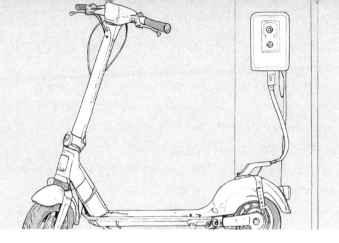

FINDING YOUR FULLY CHARGED SCOOTER

I n the previous chapter, we explored the winding paths of GitHub's Awesome Lists, where every project beckons like a unique scooter model, each with its own story, design, and potential journey. Now, the focus shifts from "where" to find these scooters to "which" one to ride. Selecting the right project isn't just about hopping on any scooter; it's about choosing one that resonates with your aspirations, enhancing your skillset, and leading to personal growth as a software developer.

The real challenge isn't the abundance of choices but knowing which projects to bypass. Much like you wouldn't jump on a scooter with a low battery or a flat tire, you shouldn't invest your time in a project that's stalled or neglected. That's why we're equipping you with a health checklist to assess the vitality and potential of each project. Think of this as your pre-ride inspection, ensuring your chosen project is in prime condition for a journey that will enrich your development skills.

This checklist is your roadmap in the terrain of open source, guiding you to projects that promise a rewarding ride. Selecting a project with momentum, support, and longevity is like choosing a fully charged scooter for your adventure through Software Development City. It ensures a fulfilling experience where you'll contribute significantly and gain valuable skills.

To demonstrate our evaluation method, let's delve into a project promoting sustainable coding practices – the Green Metrics Tool (Screenshot 6). This example will be a practical guide, teaching you how to evaluate a project's health and relevance. By analyzing this project, you'll acquire skills to assess any open-source project, ensuring you select one that excites you and fosters your growth as a developer.

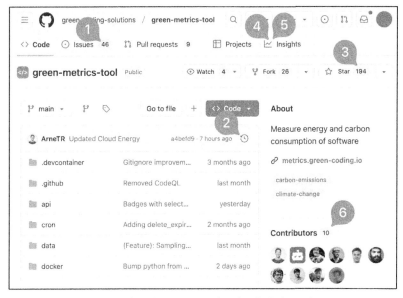

Screenshot 6: An example of a GitHub project.
https://github.com/green-coding-solutions/green-metrics-tool

Here's a list of essential factors to consider when selecting an open-source project:

1. **Issues to Tackle:** First, glance at the issues list. There should be open issues to which you can potentially contribute, ensuring there's work to be done. This can be seen directly on the project's main page (Screenshot 6).

2. **Activity and Last Commit:** A project's activity is often indicated by its last commit date. It serves as a heartbeat to show it's alive and well. A recent update, ideally within the previous week, is an excellent sign of vitality. This information is available on the main page (Screenshot 6) or by clicking Commits (Screenshot 7).

3. **Stars and Visibility:** The number of stars (Screenshot 6) a project has garnered is a testament to its community approval and visibility. A project with 10-500 stars balances recognition without being too crowded, ensuring your contributions get noticed.

4. **Pulse and Insights:** For a deeper look into the project's dynamics, the Insights section offers a snapshot of recent activities, from contributions to discussions (Screenshot 8). The Pulse subpage provides a quick health check, showing the project's activity over different time frames. Recent activities here are a good sign of a thriving project.

5. **Commit History:** Exploring the Commits tab (Screenshot 9) reveals the project's dedication and growth narrative. A consistent commit history, with regular updates, signifies a project in good health, like a scooter maintained for a smooth ride. This consistency is a hallmark of a vibrant project, offering fertile ground for your contributions.

6. **Contributor Diversity:** The number and diversity of contributors, visible from the project's main page (Screenshot 6) as well as in one of the sections of the Insights tab (Screenshot 10), reflect the community's health. A project led by a single contributor might offer unique mentorship opportunities. At the same time, a larger team suggests a collaborative environment for diverse contributions.

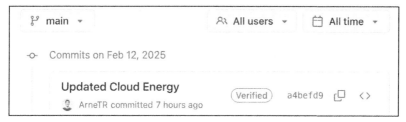

Screenshot 7: The history of commits in the GitHub project.
ttps://github.com/green-coding-solutions/green-metrics-tool/
commits/main/

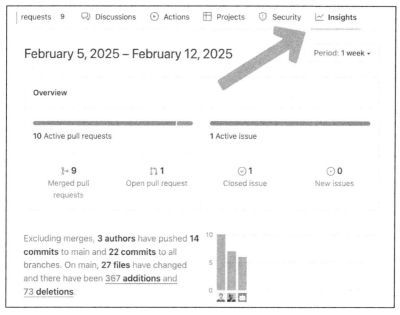

Screenshot 8: GitHub project Pulse tab.
https://github.com/green-coding-solutions/green-metrics-tool/pulse

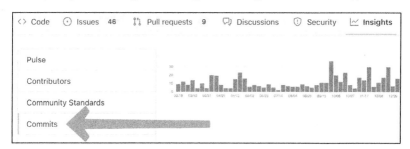

Screenshot 9: In-depth commit statistics for the GitHub project.
https://github.com/green-coding-solutions/green-metrics-tool/
graphs/commit-activity

Screenshot 10: Page displaying contributors for the GitHub project.
https://github.com/green-coding-solutions/green-metrics-tool/
graphs/contributors

This checklist protects you from investing in projects that have lost steam. You're now adept at spotting scooters with low batteries or issues, avoiding those that might stall your development journey. This ensures your contributions are welcomed and integrated, making you a valued part of the community.

However, remember that even seemingly abandoned projects can be revived. If you are interested in a dormant project, consider contacting its maintainers via an issue to inquire about its status or offer assistance. It's like jump-starting a low-battery scooter – your initiative might rekindle its life. But be cautious not to over-invest in projects showing no revival signs. Focus on those with potential for growth and collaboration.

With this knowledge, you can confidently set out on your open-source adventure, ensuring your chosen project is ready to take you the distance. Choosing the right project is crucial, but an even more critical decision awaits – selecting the right task. This choice will define the challenges you'll encounter, the skills you'll sharpen, and the impact you'll make.

STEP 3

Issue

CROSSROADS OF CONTRIBUTIONS

S o, you've discovered a fantastic open-source project – like a shiny new scooter ready to hop on! But where do you begin? The sheer number of potential issues can feel overwhelming, like standing at a busy intersection with traffic lights flashing in every direction. The key is to avoid analysis paralysis. Don't get stuck searching for the perfect first step. Instead, take a moment to look around, make sure your scooter is in good shape, and then give it a try.

How do you choose the right path? Don't underestimate small actions. Start with simple tasks to gain experience while making valuable contributions. Each fix, improved line of code, and documentation update matters. Like drops of water filling a reservoir, every contribution enhances the project. You're building momentum and progressing the project goals.

In the world of open source, there's room for everyone, from beginners to seasoned contributors. This journey is more than coding; it's about exploring interests, building skills, and making an impact. Like any adventure, expect twists and turns. As long as you stay engaged, embrace new experiences, and maintain your scooter, you will succeed. So, what kind of traffic lights can you expect to see? Here's a breakdown of the options you'll encounter:

NO CODING NEEDED:

- **Documentation:** Think of this as crafting the user manual for our scooter. You can contribute by writing clear instructions, creating tutorials, or explaining how different parts of the project function. It's also incredibly helpful to fix typos and improve formatting. This is a fantastic way to start contributing, even without coding knowledge.
- **Design:** For those with an artistic flair, you can make a significant impact by designing user-friendly interfaces or creating eye-catching logos. Your design skills can enhance a project's overall appeal and usability.

TESTING THE WATERS:

- **Testing:** This involves taking the project for a spin to ensure everything runs smoothly. You can help by identifying bugs or verifying that new features don't cause issues. To start, simply run the project, set up the environment, and explore how it works and how it's intended to work. This will help you understand its inner workings.
- **Adding unit tests:** This is a more focused approach to testing, where you write automated tests that check the functionality of specific code sections. It's a crucial step in software development, and understanding it is essential. Don't worry if it's new to you; your AI companion can help guide you. In fact, AI is great at writing unit tests.

CODING ADVENTURES:

- **Bug fixing:** Here, you'll dive into the codebase to identify and fix errors, similar to patching a leak in your scooter's tire. If you find an issue during testing, you can try to fix it, too. This is a great way to learn how code works in practice and contribute to the project's stability.

- **Code improvements:** Like tuning up your scooter, you'll make the code more efficient, readable, and maintainable. This is for more experienced developers who understand software development principles.

- **New feature implementation:** This involves designing and building brand-new functionalities for the project, like adding a sidecar to your scooter. It requires a deep understanding of the code and the project's goals, but it's also an extremely rewarding type of contribution.

STEERING THE SHIP:

- **Project management:** You will take on the role of traffic controller, coordinating tasks, managing teams, and ensuring the project stays on course. This is a significant responsibility but offers an incredible opportunity to develop leadership and organizational skills.

ΔΔΔ

The beauty of the world of open source is that you can begin your journey at any of these intersections, depending on your interests and skills. If you're new to this, focus on those easy green lights, like documentation or simple bug fixes. These will help you gain confidence before tackling more complex tasks. The aim is to continuously move forward by exploring new paths, trying different things, and never hesitating to ask for help. The open-source community is full of welcoming people ready to share their knowledge and help you grow. In the upcoming chapters, we'll explore how GitHub labels issues for beginners and utilize AI to assist in this process.

STICKER SCAVENGER HUNT

R emember those stickers we saw plastered all over the scooters? The ones that seemed a bit random at first? It turns out they're not just for show. They're actually helpful guides pointing us toward the right open-source projects for our skills and interests.

And those stickers aren't just on scooters, either. They're everywhere, even at the traffic lights! While they might initially look like random graffiti, each sticker signifies a specific type of task awaiting you: fixing a bug, adding a new feature, or testing code. Some are common across the city, while others are project-specific. They offer a way to find the perfect starting point for your first contribution.

For newcomers like us, the most essential sticker to look for is the Good First Issue label. It's like a green light, an open invitation saying, *"This task is perfect for beginners!"* It's your entry point to making your first contribution.

So, how do you find these beginner-friendly opportunities? Projects usually have a Contribute page (Screenshot 11). It shows a curated list of issues, often labeled Good First Issue. This is your gateway to projects that actively welcome new contributors and offer tasks suited to your initial skillset.

Digging deeper into a project's structure, you'll find the Issues tab. Think of this as a directory of current tasks and challenges. Here, you can filter issues using labels like Good First Issue or Beginner. Just pop *is:open label:"Good First Issue"* into the search bar to quickly locate suitable tasks (Screenshot 12).

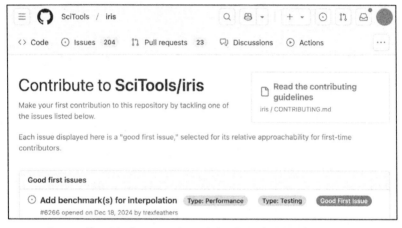

Screenshot 11: A screenshot of the GitHub Contribute page.
https://github.com/SciTools/iris/contribute

Screenshot 12: This image shows the GitHub Issues page.
https://github.com/SciTools/iris/labels/Good%20First%20Issue

The Good First Issue label is more than just a tag; it's a welcoming signal to newcomers eager to contribute. Several online platforms act as filters and guides to streamline your search, highlighting projects that embrace first-time contributors. These act like specialized maps, leading you straight to the Good First Issue opportunities. Let's take a look at some of them:

- climatetriage.com: Here, climate change activism meets software development, all through the lens of Good First Issues. This site focuses on open-source projects related to climate and sustainability, and it also categorizes projects by programming language.

- www.firsttimersonly.com: This site is a haven for beginners, curating beginner-friendly projects alongside guides and advice for first-time contributors. It's your go-to resource for navigating the initial complexities of open source.

- up-for-grabs.net: This platform aggregates projects that actively seek contributors. Look for labels like *up-for-grabs, jump-in,* or *help wanted* to find projects where your contributions are welcomed.

- goodfirstissues.com: This site aggregates the most recent Good First Issue tagged issues from across GitHub. It's a fantastic resource for finding manageable tasks that match your skills.

- goodfirstissue.dev: This platform carefully selects easy tasks from established open-source projects, offering a focused path for those just starting.

- www.codetriage.com: This platform will send you a new open issue from your favorite projects directly to your inbox daily, helping you stay connected and contribute regularly.

Think of these platforms as well-informed guides, pointing you toward neighborhoods where you can make a real difference. By using these resources, you're not just finding any project;

you're finding a community that values and appreciates your contributions, no matter how small they seem.

Another great trick for finding beginner-friendly projects is searching GitHub using the good-first-issue topic[32]. This is like finding a parking lot full of scooters, all sporting the welcoming sticker! Projects using this topic are specifically designed to onboard newcomers with guidance and support. These are like training wheels for your coding journey, providing a safe place to learn and contribute to real-world projects.

Finding your niche in this vast city requires a mix of topic searching and exploring projects that catch your eye. Once you've identified a topic that excites you, it's time to visit the project's Contribute page. Here, you'll find the list of tasks that show where your skills can be used.

Exciting, isn't it? The world of open source is filled with opportunities and built with newcomers in mind. The sheer number of resources dedicated to guiding you underscores the supportive nature of the software development community. It's like having a community of experienced riders cheering you on as you start your journey.

So, are you ready to rev your engines and start your open-source adventure? We'll delve into the contribution process in the next chapters, guiding you step-by-step. You'll learn to read project documentation, collaborate effectively with other developers, and gain all the tools you need to make meaningful contributions. Prepare to put your skills to the test and find the joy of creating something that matters. Your open-source journey awaits!

---

[32] https://github.com/topics/good-first-issue

STEP 4
Contribution

THE BACKBONE OF CONTRIBUTION

Y ou've mastered the navigation theory, weaving your way through the bustling streets of Software Development City. But hold on tight because we're about to unlock the contribution stage – your chance to take the world of open source for a spin, even before you've earned your full developer's license.

Before you embark on your open-source journey, it's crucial to understand the concept of contributions and the tools that power this world. Imagine contributions as your chance to personalize your ride and tweak and enhance the very software that makes this city run. It's your opportunity to leave your mark, to help others navigate the streets with greater ease, and to build something that benefits the entire community. But just as tuning an engine requires understanding its components, making meaningful contributions requires mastering the tools underpinning the world of open source.

The Version Control System (VCS) is the most essential of these tools. It allows you to track changes, collaborate with others, and revert to previous versions if something goes wrong. In Software

Development City, there's one VCS that's as ubiquitous as scooters themselves: Git[33].

Picture Git as the odometer on your electric scooter. Just as the odometer tracks your mileage, Git meticulously records every twist and turn in your project's development. Every line of code you write, every bug you squash, every feature you add – it's all logged in Git's detailed history. This isn't just a neat feature; it's a lifesaver. Imagine accidentally introducing a bug that throws your entire codebase into disarray. With Git, you can simply rewind to a previous, bug-free version, like hitting the reset button on your scooter's journey.

But Git isn't just for solo rides. The true magic of open-source development lies in collaboration. Git acts as the central communication hub, allowing everyone to see each other's changes, avoid conflicts, and ultimately merge their individual contributions into a single, improved version.

Git acts as a safety net. Did you accidentally delete a crucial file or make a disruptive change? Don't panic! Git serves as a backup, allowing effortless restoration of previous versions. It's like having a spare tire for your scooter, letting you experiment without fearing irreparable damage.

Git is your playground for innovation. If you want to test a new feature without disrupting the project, create a branch to experiment without affecting the main codebase. It's like a secret test track for your scooter; you can push it to the limits and try new modifications. Merging back into the main project is as easy as merging onto the highway road.

Git is more than a Version Control System; it's the backbone of open-source collaboration and a key to your potential as a developer. In the next chapter, we'll explore how Git enables precise and impactful contributions to open-source projects. Prepare to learn a tool that professional developers use every day.

---

[33] https://git-scm.com/videos

PIMP MY RIDE

In the last chapter, we got acquainted with Git, the backbone of open-source contributions. Now, it's time to get our hands dirty in the open-source workshop and understand the practical side of Git. Think of your project like an electric scooter, safely stored in a central garage – this garage is your repository, or "repo" for short. It's a sophisticated storage facility that houses every version of your scooter and keeps a meticulous record of its evolution, like a super-charged odometer. Don't worry about installing Git just yet; we'll get to that in the next chapter. For now, let's focus on understanding the key concepts[34].

Now, you wouldn't want to start taking apart your scooter in the middle of a busy street, would you? That's where your working directory comes in. It's your personal workspace, a safe haven to freely tinker with your scooter (your project's code). Here, you can experiment, fix bugs, and add new features without affecting the main project. Think of it as having a garage where you can freely tinker.

As you make changes to your scooter, it's essential to document your progress. This is where commits come into play. A

---

[34] https://git-scm.com/docs/gittutorial

`git commit` is like taking a snapshot of your project at a specific moment. It captures the current state of your code and includes a brief description of the changes you've made, providing a clear record of your modifications.

Imagine you've safely stored your project in your working directory and are now ready with a brilliant idea for a new feature, like adding neon lights to your scooter. However, your hesitation to implement it directly on the project due to fears of unforeseen problems is where branches come to the rescue. A `git branch` is like creating a portal, a separate, parallel workspace for your project, where you can experiment freely without affecting the original codebase. It's like having a secret portal where you can try out those neon lights without risking damage to your main scooter.

Once you've perfected your neon light installation, it's time to integrate it back into the main project. This is where the `git merge` command comes in handy. It seamlessly combines your changes from the branch into the main codebase, like attaching your shiny new neon lights to your original scooter.

At last, after all your efforts, it's time to introduce your enhanced scooter to everyone. This is the moment when the `git push` command is needed. It's like rolling your upgraded scooter out of the garage and onto the streets, making your contributions visible to other developers. On the flip side, if you want to see what others have been up to, you can use `git pull` to download their changes to your local workspace. It's like peeking into other developers' garages to see what modifications they've made to their scooters.

By understanding these core Git concepts, you'll unlock the power to make tangible contributions to the world of open source using the same tools professional developers rely on daily.

Get ready because in the next chapter, we'll dive into a hands-on test drive. You'll experiment with these Git commands on a safe, practice project – a test dummy scooter if you will. This experience will solidify your understanding of Git and prepare you to confidently contribute to real open-source projects. Get ready to learn something new and start your journey into the bustling city of software development!

THE DUMMY SCOOTER

Y ou've explored the fundamentals of Git – its key concepts, commands, and mechanics. It's time to take your first real steps into the world of open source by practicing those skills. Theory is essential, but nothing beats hands-on experience, and that's why we need the Dummy Scooter project. This First Contributions[35] repository is a sandbox created specifically for beginners to test their Git skills in a safe, pressure-free environment. Think of it as your first solo ride, but with training wheels that you can take off whenever you're ready.

As you prepare to dive in, the Quest Helper – a magical white cat with glowing emerald eyes – appears by your side. With a flick of his tail, he gives you an encouraging look.

"This is your moment to step out on your own," he says with a mischievous grin. "The first steps can feel a little wobbly, but trust me, you've got this. Open the Dummy Scooter repository and follow its instructions. The journey will be much more exciting when you're the one steering."

---

[35] https://github.com/firstcontributions/first-contributions

With that, he leaps onto a nearby fence and disappears, leaving you to take the lead. It's up to you now – but don't worry, you've been given the tools to succeed.

Instead of relying on the book to spoon-feed instructions, the real task is to follow the guide directly. Open the First Contributions repository and get started. It's a perfect opportunity to interact with an actual GitHub project, learn its workflows, and see open-source collaboration in action. This guide provides a step-by-step walkthrough designed for newcomers just like you.

The first step is to ensure Git is installed on your computer. If you haven't done that yet, set up Git right now[36].

Here's an overview of what you'll be doing next, but don't expect exact screenshots or exhaustive steps from this chapter. The real challenge – and joy – is learning to navigate these processes independently:

- **Fork and Clone the Repository:** Imagine forking as creating your personal workspace – a place where you can make changes freely. After forking, clone the repository to your local machine using Git. This lets you work offline, giving you the freedom to explore without fear of breaking anything.

- **Create a Branch:** Your branch is your own private lane of development. By branching off, you isolate your work from the main project. For this exercise, you'll create a branch specifically to add your name to the `CONTRIBUTORS.md` file.

- **Make Changes:** Open the `CONTRIBUTORS.md` file in a text editor and add your name. Keep it simple and professional – this is your first mark in the world of open source.

- **Commit Your Work:** A commit is like stamping your approval on the changes. Write a clear message describing your update (e.g., *Added [your name] to CONTRIBUTORS.md*).

---

[36] https://docs.github.com/en/get-started/getting-started-with-git/set-up-git

- **Submit a Pull Request:** This is the exciting part. Push your branch to your forked repository on GitHub and create a pull request. It's your formal proposal to integrate your changes into the main project. Once your pull request is submitted, a special maintainer bot will review it. Don't be intimidated; it's all part of the process. In your future projects, reviews will be performed by real maintainers, and most of them are welcoming, especially to first-timers. You may even receive feedback to help you improve.

The Quest Helper reappears, perched high on a nearby post. "Feeling unsure? That's normal," he says, yawning lazily. "But you've already taken the hardest step – getting started. If you hit a bump, ask your favorite AI assistant first. If that doesn't help, search for solutions online next. You'll find a wealth of resources and forums filled with people who've been in your shoes."

The cat flicks his ears toward the horizon. "Now, stop reading and start doing. The Dummy Scooter awaits!" With a final stretch, he vanishes again, leaving you to tackle this quest on your own.

The best part of this experience is that you'll not only learn Git in practice but also earn a tangible result: your name will be added to the contributors' Hall of Fame. It's a small yet significant milestone – a reminder of where your journey into open source began.

FILL THE BLANK PAGE

Congratulations on successfully navigating the Dummy Scooter project! You've taken a significant step towards becoming an open-source contributor. Before we start our first real task, let's look at how we learn and grow. An important part of this journey is keeping track of your progress.

Don't be discouraged if you are lost in a maze of unfamiliar terms and concepts. This initial disorientation is a sign of new territory waiting to be explored. If everything made perfect sense immediately, there would be no room for growth. Embrace the confusion, questions, and feeling overwhelmed; they are all part of the learning process, the stepping stones on your path to mastery.

As you embark on this journey, make a point to record your experiences, your triumphs, and your struggles. Writing is a powerful tool whether you prefer the sleek interface of digital notetaking apps like Notion[37], Obsidian[38], or the open-source alternative Logseq[39], or the tactile feel of a worn notebook[40]. It helps you

---

[37] https://www.notion.com/
[38] https://obsidian.md/
[39] https://github.com/logseq/logseq
[40] https://greenlightcareer.tech/book/notebook

organize your thoughts, solidify your understanding, and track your progress.

By capturing ideas in a trusted system, whether it's through mind mapping in XMind[41], the Cornell notetaking method, or the flexible Zettelkasten system, you're building a personal knowledge management system that grows with you. Some developers have found success with the PARA method (Projects, Areas, Resources, Archives) in organizing their technical documentation. What matters most is finding a system that resonates with your workflow and helps you maintain momentum in your open-source journey. For more detailed insights into these notetaking methods and how to adapt them to your development workflow, visit my website[42], where I explore notetaking and productivity systems designed specifically for developers.

Organize your notes before you begin coding and take a moment to review the chapter on project health to take some notes. Recall the indicators of a thriving project: a steady stream of commits, an active and engaged community, and responsive maintainers. Remember, a healthy project ensures a smooth and enjoyable ride, just like a well-maintained scooter. Make some notes about Git, too, to keep all your new knowledge close at hand.

With your knowledge toolkit and your chosen project in hand, you're ready for the next step. Be aware that the road ahead will present challenges. In the next chapter, we'll explore the nuances of navigating the pathways of open-source contributions, uncovering valuable insights, and avoiding potential pitfalls. Get ready to accelerate learning, expand your skills, and make your mark in software development.

---

[41] https://xmind.app/
[42] https://greenlightcareer.tech/book/notes

FROM BLACK BOXES TO
BUILDING BLOCKS

H aving identified a potential project and some Good First Issues to tackle, it's time to shift from theory to action. In
the previous chapter, we discussed the importance of notetaking
for your learning process. Now, what's next? Where do you start,
and what should you document?

The answer lies in starting at the tip of the iceberg – with the
task itself. First, you must understand what to do, and only then
can you explore how to do it. This is where your AI companion
comes into play. Think of it as asking a local for directions before
venturing into unfamiliar territory.

To begin, find a chatbot that can work with internet resources
or an assistant capable of viewing your screen. Remember to visit
my website[43] for up-to-date guides on available AI tools as new
assistants emerge frequently.

Share your chosen project link and the specific issue you want
to address. Start with broad by asking, *"What does this issue en-
tail?"* or *"What is the goal of this task?"*. Don't hesitate to ask

---

[43] https://greenlightcareer.tech/book/blackbox

seemingly simple questions; there are no dumb questions when you're learning something new, and your AI companion is always ready to help. If the assistant struggles to grasp the broader context, go to the project's main page and documentation, share your screen, and repeat your questions. Your task is to do research and gather as many clues as possible.

Be bold and persistent in your conversation with the AI. You don't need to worry about being polite or bothering your AI friend. It's there to help you, so ask away! If something needs clarification, rephrase your questions or ask them from a different angle. Your AI companion is infinitely patient and will gladly repeat information until you understand.

As you converse with your AI assistant, take short notes on your findings, focusing on the overall picture. If you are getting bogged down in specifics, step back and consider the project as a whole.

But AI isn't omniscient. Traditional search engines like Google will often be your best resource. By merging AI's power with reliable search techniques, you can find answers to complex questions.

In programming, black box[44] is a valuable concept. It means focusing on what a component does (its input and output) without worrying about how it works internally. This approach allows you to grasp the overall structure of a new project without getting lost in details.

Imagine exploring a complex machine where each part acts like a black box. Understanding how each part works takes time, but this understanding allows you to grasp the bigger picture and see how all parts work together. Document your findings as you go. If you run out of time, simply bookmark where you left off and save your conversation with your AI assistant, allowing you to return later.

---

[44] https://en.wikipedia.org/wiki/Black_box

105

Once you have a clearer understanding of what needs to be accomplished, you can move on to the next phase. Surface-level analysis may not always be enough. If you believe that you have covered all the essential concepts and identified the complex areas, it's time to dive deeper into the code. Your first step will likely be setting up the project locally on your computer.

In the next chapter, we'll continue our conversation with the AI assistant, focusing on precisely that.

NAVIGATING THE SCOOTER HANDBOOK

I n the previous chapter, we explored the black box approach to understanding a project, where you gathered high-level information without diving into the code. Now, it's time to get hands-on and set up your local development environment – your personal workshop where you'll build and test your contributions. We'll transition from the conceptual to the practical, starting with a review of what you've already done and moving on to the actual project.

You've already experienced the core workflow with the dummy scooter project: forking the repository, cloning it to your machine, and creating a dedicated branch for your changes. It's time to apply these skills to your chosen open-source project. This time, though, your contributions will have a real impact.

Before jumping into the real project's codebase, let's revisit those crucial steps we took with the dummy scooter. If you recall, we forked the repository on GitHub, created a local copy using `git clone`, and then created a branch to contain our changes using `git checkout -b your-branch-name`. These steps are fundamental to open-source contribution, and you'll use them every time.

The very first step in contributing to any project will look similar. First, you'll need to fork the repository of the project you chose on GitHub and then clone it locally using the `git clone` command.

Before you begin making any changes, it's essential to understand how the project expects contributions to be made. This is where the project documentation becomes important. You'll want to locate the `CONTRIBUTING.md` file. This file is often found at the root of the repository or is linked from `README.md`. This document is your project's guide to best practices, outlining the project's community rules, coding standards, and workflow. It's like the assembly manual for your scooter, providing a crucial guide. The `CONTRIBUTING.md` file will often detail the preferred way to submit your work, ensuring it integrates smoothly with the existing code.

Next, you'll want to find the Get Started guide. Sometimes, this is part of the `CONTRIBUTING.md` file, but often, it is a separate document or a page linked from the `README.md`. This guide acts as your entry point for setting up a local environment. It will walk you through the project's tech stack, required software, and how to set up your development environment. Think of it as getting familiar with the controls and features of your scooter.

You'll want to ensure you have the right tools, like Node.js or Python, and understand the project's purpose. Many projects use Docker[45] for containerization, so it's worth speaking with your AI assistant about core Docker concepts and filling your notes with knowledge about this crucial development tool.

It's a good idea to search for more detailed documentation links and to familiarize yourself with the documentation table of contents. Don't try to read everything at the moment. Just be aware of what is there and can be helpful.

---

[45] https://docs.docker.com/get-started/docker-overview/

The Get Started guide often contains detailed steps on setting up dependencies, compiling code, and running unit tests[46]. As you set up your environment, pay particular attention to instructions regarding unit testing and automated tests. These tests ensure your contributions do not introduce bugs or break existing functionality.

It's crucial to understand that every project is unique, with its own quirks and specific requirements, just like each scooter is different. The CONTRIBUTING.md and Get Started guides are tailored to the project's goals. Take your time to read them thoroughly, using your AI companion to help clarify anything you don't fully understand. The better you know your chosen project, the more effective and confident you will be in your contributions.

You should also look for links to community resources such as Discord, forums, or chat groups. These are crucial to engaging with other developers and getting help when needed. Don't hesitate to contact them if you have questions or encounter difficulties during the setup process.

With your development environment humming and your contribution branch ready, it's time to delve into Integrated Development Environments. In the next chapter, we'll explore their functionalities and how they'll become your go-to tools for modifying your selected project and leaving your impact on the open-source community!

---

[46] https://en.wikipedia.org/wiki/Unit_testing

WELCOME TO THE GEAR SHOP

W ith your project now set up on your local machine, ready for contributions, it's time to equip yourself with the right tools for the job. Software development is all about writing, managing, and understanding code, the very essence of bringing projects to life. To navigate this code effectively, you need a suitable environment. This is where Integrated Development Environments (IDEs)[47] come into play, your personal mechanic's toolbox from the Gear Shop – another open-source awesome list[48].

Imagine pulling your freshly acquired electric scooter into a bustling workshop. The air is filled with the hum of tools and the clang of metal. Here, you'll find the magic of coding. Just as a mechanic wouldn't tackle an engine overhaul with bare hands, you won't modify intricate code without the proper tools. Think of IDEs as power tools for coding, making development easier and your code more robust.

---

[47] https://en.wikipedia.org/wiki/Integrated_development_environment
[48] https://github.com/zeelsheladiya/Awesome-IDEs

A seasoned shopkeeper greets you. His wisdom is evident in his warm smile. "Welcome to the Gear Shop," he says, his voice resonating through the space. "Every developer needs the right tools for the job, and I've got just what you need."

He shows you around, pointing to various toolboxes under the bright lights. "These aren't ordinary toolboxes," he explains. "They're IDEs, the coding world's power tools."

As you explore, he shares insights on key IDE features:

- **Syntax Highlighting:** Like seeing your scooter's wiring lit up in different colors for easy identification, syntax highlighting makes code more readable by color-coding elements like functions and variables.

- **Code Completion:** When you're stuck, this feature acts like an assistant, suggesting the names of functions or variables as you type, saving time and reducing errors.

- **Debugging:** Here, you can think of debugging as using a magnifying glass to inspect your code closely, helping you find and fix errors more efficiently.

Excited by these capabilities, you're eager to choose your IDE. The shopkeeper praises Visual Studio Code's[49] versatility, "With the right extensions, it's an excellent choice for any programming language, and it's free and open-source, showcasing the strength of community-driven development." He then adds, "For those looking for AI assistance directly within their coding environment, consider Cursor[50]. It's built on VS Code, so you'll feel right at home, but it integrates powerful AI features to help you write code faster and more efficiently. It's a paid product, but the AI assistance can be a real game-changer." He points to a flowchart on a whiteboard, guiding you through selecting the proper IDE based on the programming language.

---

[49] https://code.visualstudio.com/
[50] https://www.cursor.com/

For your Python-focused project, he recommends PyCharm[51], "A dream for Python developers, packed with Python-specific features." If your project includes Java, he suggests Eclipse[52] or IntelliJ IDEA[53], "Both are powerhouses for Java development, enhancing your coding with advanced features."

If you're still unsure, your AI companion can provide further guidance. Simply show or describe the languages used in your project (you might even insert a screenshot of the language profile from the GitHub main page here), and your AI can suggest IDEs based on functionality and your preferences.

For those eager to explore more, the digital world offers plenty of resources, including my website[54], which provides a comprehensive guide to IDEs and their capabilities.

Equipped with this knowledge, you're now ready to select your IDE, set up your coding workstation, and dive into your open-source contribution adventure.

---

[51] https://www.jetbrains.com/pycharm/
[52] https://eclipseide.org/
[53] https://www.jetbrains.com/idea/
[54] https://greenlightcareer.tech/book/ide

CODE CRIME SCENE

As you admire your newly chosen IDE in the workshop, a curious object catches your eye – a large, ornate magnifying glass. The shopkeeper, noticing your interest, explains with a knowing smile, "That's no ordinary magnifying glass, my friend. That's a debugger – an essential tool for any coder. Think of it as a detective's lens for the digital world, perfect for investigating those pesky code mysteries – bugs!"

You've made some changes, eager to see your new functionality come to life. But, alas, things aren't working as expected. Your program isn't performing correctly, throwing cryptic error messages your way. Suddenly, your code has become a crime scene, and you're the detective tasked with solving the mystery.

The shopkeeper continues with the analogy. "Like a detective arriving at a crime scene, you must first gather clues. What error messages are displayed? Does the program produce unexpected results, or does it crash? These are your initial digital fingerprints, hints that something has gone wrong."

He leans in, lowering his voice, "Next comes the interrogation – scrutinizing your code. You'll need to examine each line, look for inconsistencies, and try to understand the program's path before the error. This includes examining the state of your variables at different stages and exploring the application's memory."

Sometimes, just looking at the code isn't enough. This is where the debugger, your most potent tool, becomes essential. Integrated directly into your IDE, it allows you to step through your code line by line, observe the values of your variables at each step, and understand how the program is functioning at a much more granular level.

Think of it like having a transparent view into the mind of your program. You can slow it down and observe how each instruction influences its state. This powerful feature can quickly reveal hidden logic errors or unexpected behavior.

Aside from the debugger, there are other valuable tools you might need, such as:

- **Print Statements:** Consider them temporary beepers that can be placed strategically within your code. When executed, the program will output a message indicating the line is being processed, helping you to track the flow of execution.

- **File Logs:** These act like detailed logbooks, recording the program's activities. File logs capture the execution flow, variable changes, and messages output by your program.

- **Error Stack Traces:** Contained within the logs, these are a record of how an error (the crime) was triggered. They detail the sequence of function calls leading up to the error and the exact line of code where it occurred. This makes it much faster to pinpoint where the issue resides.

Once you've gathered enough evidence and identified the bug, it's time to fix the code. This involves careful correction of any errors and testing to ensure that the problem is truly resolved. You'll need to run your program thoroughly, scrutinizing its behavior to verify that it functions as intended.

Debugging can be challenging but incredibly rewarding. With the right tools, a bit of perseverance, and support from the open-source community, you will transform into a skilled detective, capable of solving the most complex coding mysteries. Remember to check my website[55] for more resources, where you'll find comprehensive guides on debugging techniques for different IDEs.

No detective works in isolation. The internet is filled with experienced developers ready to assist. The project's GitHub issue page is often the best first stop when seeking help, as this is where others might have encountered and resolved similar issues. Feel free to ask questions, leveraging the collective knowledge of the open-source community.

AI chatbots can also be valuable allies in your debugging journey. If you share error stack traces with them, they can quickly identify common issues, suggest solutions, and even provide code examples. AI can help you streamline the debugging process and solve problems more efficiently.

"Here," the shopkeeper says, handing you the weighty IDE toolbox, "you have all the essential tools for investigating any code crime scene. You have everything needed to track down those pesky bugs." He then picks up the ornate magnifying glass. "And with this beauty, you're now fully equipped to solve any mysteries that come your way!"

---

[55] https://greenlightcareer.tech/book/debug

POWER UP YOUR CODING

P urr-fect choice, adventurer!" your magical cat Quest Helper's eyes gleamed with enthusiasm. "It's fantastic that you decided to delve deeper into IDEs. Speaking of delving," the cat added, its whiskers twitching mischievously, "did you know there's a whole workshop dedicated to AI companions right here in Software Development City?"

Intrigued by the prospect of encountering AI assistants, you nod eagerly. "Sounds like a perfect place to explore some options!"

Your feline companion's tail swished excitedly. "That's precisely where you'll find the ideal AI partner for your coding adventures! Many awesome AI code assistants[56] gather there, each with unique functionalities just waiting to be discovered."

Following your Quest Helper's guidance, you venture deeper into Software Development City, arriving at the bustling AI Workshop. The scene is unlike anything you've encountered before. Eccentric programmers huddle over their workstations, their faces

---

[56] https://github.com/sourcegraph/awesome-code-ai

illuminated by the glow of their screens. But the real stars of the show are the AI companions themselves!

With your magical cat padding silently beside you, you navigate the workshop, eager to experiment with these fascinating tools. You test-drive various AI companions, their functionalities as diverse as their designs. Your eyes widen as you discover GitHub Copilot[57], which not only offers lightning-fast code completion but can also review your Pull Requests and even change multiple files on your request. Suddenly, writing code feels more like a collaborative effort, your skills amplified by Copilot's knowledge.

But the true magic unfolds as you delve deeper. "Why don't you try Gemini?" your Quest Helper suggests with a knowing purr. Stuck on a particularly challenging task? Your Quest Helper suggests asking Gemini Code Assist[58] directly, and to your IDE, it conjures up a solution! The AI acts like a contextual wizard, weaving its digital expertise by scouring your project files and open-source resources for relevant code examples or tutorials that perfectly address your coding hurdle.

"Lost in a sea of Google search results? Ah, this is where Tabnine[59] shines," your magical cat says, leading you to this specialized chatbot integrated into your IDE that takes your natural language description of a problem and translates it into effective search queries, finding the most relevant solutions from Stack Overflow[60] or other developer forums. Moreover, Tabnine can also check your Pull Requests[61], offering suggestions for improvements. "Think of it as having a master librarian at your disposal," purrs your Quest Helper.

---

[57] https://github.com/features/copilot
[58] https://cloud.google.com/products/gemini/code-assist
[59] https://www.tabnine.com/
[60] https://stackoverflow.com/
[61] https://www.tabnine.com/blog/unveiling-tabnines-code-review-agent

Intrigued by the vast array of AI functionalities, you turn to your magical companion. "Is there a comprehensive guide to all these amazing AI tools?" you inquire.

"Meow-st certainly, adventurer!" your Quest Helper replies, its emerald eyes twinkling. "You'll find a constantly updated list of the latest and greatest AI companions, along with detailed breakdowns of their features, on Dan's website[62]. Feel free to subscribe for updates on the ever-evolving world of AI coding assistants!"

By the end of your visit to the AI Workshop, you've discovered the perfect AI companion for your coding journey and unlocked a powerful new ally in your quest to become a contributing member of the open-source community. With your mystical feline guide showing you the way and a fully equipped coding workstation at your disposal, you're well on your way to making a tangible impact on the software development landscape.

---

[62] https://greenlightcareer.tech/book/ai

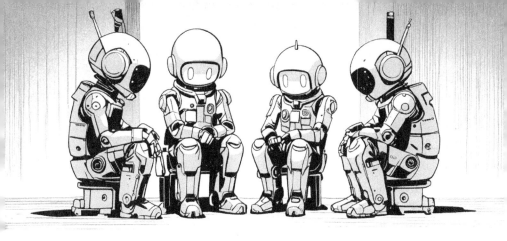

EXPLORING THE AI FRONTIER

A s you are about to leave the vibrant AI Workshop, a new wave of curiosity washes over you. In a corner of the workshop, you notice a group of chatbots huddled together, their digital voices buzzing with animated conversation.

"Fascinating, wouldn't you say?" your Quest Helper purrs, its emerald eyes glowing with interest. "These are browser-based AI chatbots and extensions designed to work seamlessly within your web browser." Your magical cat's tail swishes thoughtfully as it leads you closer.

You approach the group eager to learn more. One chatbot's interface, adorned with friendly blue chat bubbles, explains its unique functionality. "Unlike companions that reside within your IDE," it chirps, "we can actually read and understand the content of the web pages you visit! Think of us as digital librarians, able to parse information and offer assistance directly on your browser."

The possibilities spark your imagination. "Could these chatbots help with open-source contributions?" you ask eagerly.

"Precisely!" another chatbot chimes in, its voice filled with enthusiasm. Your Quest Helper nods sagely as the chatbot continues: "Imagine tackling a simple documentation issue on a project's GitHub repository. With specific browser-based AI tools, like Microsoft Copilot[63] integrated with Edge, you could open the issue directly on GitHub and ask Copilot to suggest a solution (Screenshot 13). Copilot, analyzing the context of the issue and the surrounding code, might suggest adding comments to the code to clarify the intended behavior of the cache argument or even propose potential code modifications to make the cache functionality work as expected."

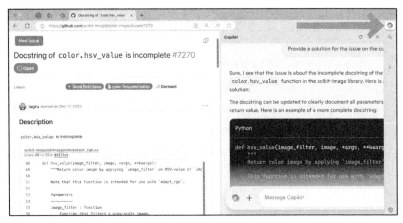

Screenshot 13: An example of the solution suggested by MS Edge Copilot.
https://github.com/scikit-image/scikit-image/issues/7270

If you prefer using Google Chrome, an alternative could be the Perplexity[64] AI extension, which also supports web page summarization and search.

The implications are astounding. Browser-based chatbots provide a new level of accessibility, allowing engagement with open-source projects and contributions without active coding. However, they lack broader context and can only summarize current page content, making them effective primarily for simple issues.

---

[63] https://www.microsoft.com/en-us/edge/features/copilot
[64] https://www.perplexity.ai/

Generally, they excel at summarizing issues and searching the internet behalf.

A thirst for further knowledge consumes you. "Is this all I need to know about AI in the world of open source, or is there anything else I should be aware of?" you ask, glancing at your feline guide.

Your magical cat's whiskers twitch with excitement. "The realm of AI in open source extends beyond the helpful companions you've encountered today," it purrs thoughtfully, padding around the workshop's corner. "On the cutting edge of development, researchers are exploring the potential of AI agents that can work autonomously within a project's codebase. Imagine a tireless digital assistant scouring the code for inefficiencies or potential improvements and suggesting modifications!"

Your mind races with possibilities. "That sounds incredible! Are there any real-world examples of this technology in action?"

"Meow indeed!" your Quest Helper's tail perks up enthusiastically. "One such project is called SWE-agent, currently under development[65]. While still in its early stages, SWE-agent represents a glimpse into the future of AI-powered open-source development. In this future, intelligent agents collaborate alongside human coders to create even more efficient and robust software."

This revelation ignites a fire within you. With AI support in your IDE and within the codebase, the possibilities for real impact seem limitless. With a newfound appreciation for AI's potential in open source, you're ready to dive in.

The next chapter will guide you through exploring the codebase, understanding its functionalities, and finding your first contribution. Get ready to collaborate with the community, leverage your AI companions, and make a lasting impact on the open-source ecosystem!

---

[65] https://github.com/princeton-nlp/SWE-agent

CONQUERING YOUR
FIRST TRAFFIC LIGHT

The AI Workshop fades behind you, leaving a trail of neon lights and buzzing conversations. As you retrace your steps, the digital guidance of your AI companion leads you back to where your journey began – to the traffic lights representing the issues you've chosen to tackle in your open-source contribution. The goal is to stay focused on this initial task, using all the tools you've gathered to make progress. It's not just about abstract learning; it's about using that learning to make a concrete contribution.

This phase requires a deep dive. Your mission is to understand the codebase's language, pinpoint the issue's location, and develop a solution. Consider it like deciphering a complex puzzle, unlocking the mysteries of the software. You are not starting from scratch anymore. The AI assistants and your coding toolbox are at your disposal. If you encounter a function or variable you don't understand, use your AI partners to explore the code, illuminating the connections and details of each puzzle piece.

As you delve deeper, your new knowledge and the guidance of your AI companions will pay dividends. Ideas that once seemed opaque will gradually reveal their workings.

However, there will be times when you get stuck, facing a particularly tricky section of code. This is a natural part of the process, where a Draft Pull Request becomes your most valuable tool. Think of it as a signal flare, alerting other developers that you need assistance.

Creating a helpful draft PR[66] is like drawing a detailed map. In the title, clearly and concisely state the problem you're tackling: *"Help Needed: Debugging [Function Name] in [File Name]"*, for example. The PR description details the steps you've taken, including relevant code snippets and error messages you have encountered. This helps others retrace your steps, understand your thought process, and offer informed help. Don't be shy, state that you are *"looking for feedback on my approach"* or *"need guidance to move forward."* This clarifies your intention and encourages collaboration.

Here's where the magic of open source unfolds. When you create a draft PR, experienced developers from the project may offer comments, suggest solutions, point you to helpful resources, or propose alternative approaches.

This collaborative journey will enable you to find the missing piece and craft a solution to your chosen problem. You will update your code, integrate the feedback, and submit your PR for review. This will be a significant accomplishment, but the final push will be yours. It will be up to you to take the guidance you receive and translate it into a working solution tailored to the specific needs of the issue. There won't be one correct path; the journey will depend on the chosen task, so the final steps will always be yours.

It's important not to get caught up waiting passively for a response to your PR. While that process unfolds, immediately seek another challenge, another opportunity to contribute to the same project or even a new one. Keep this momentum going. But don't feel rushed. The journey of learning software development and open source is not a sprint. It's a marathon. Some tasks might take an hour, while others might take days or weeks. Your progress is not measured in the speed of delivery. Still, in the depth of understanding you gain and your growth as a contributor.

Embrace the challenges, utilize your tools, and keep on learning. Each challenge you address and each problem you solve builds your skills and strengthens your confidence. With every step, you're not just contributing to open-source projects. You're building your future.

The world of open source is full of opportunities, awaiting your unique perspective and skills. The final solution is in your hands. Are you ready to take the next step and create it?

GREENLIGHT MINDSET

Y ou've faced your first challenge and made it through! It wasn't a sprint but a focused effort requiring persistence, and you conquered it. Whether your contribution was a minor code fix or a deeper exploration, you took that crucial step forward, a victory worth celebrating. Take a moment to appreciate that accomplishment! You're actively contributing to real-world software, which already makes you a developer!

However, the path ahead is not always clear. There will be times when, despite your best efforts, your contributions might not be immediately accepted. The project maintainers might suggest alternative solutions, or you might realize you need a deeper understanding of the codebase. Don't let this discourage you. Even if it seems critical, feedback is incredibly valuable for future progress. Analyze the suggestions from experienced developers, understand their rationale, and use this knowledge as a stepping stone to refine your skills. Every piece of feedback is a lesson learned. Remember, even if your first attempt wasn't immediately merged, you've gained valuable insights that will make you more effective the next time.

If a particular project consistently poses challenges, don't feel obligated to stay on that path. The vast landscape of open source offers countless projects across a multitude of technologies and interests. Perhaps a different project will better align with your skills and spark a new passion. Explore, experiment, and find the open-source projects that ignite your coding drive. Maybe you realize that the initial programming language or topic you chose isn't quite what you imagined. This is perfectly fine! The world of open source thrives on exploration and experimentation. Use this journey to broaden your horizons. You might uncover a hidden passion for a completely new area of software development. There are countless opportunities to learn, try new things, and refine your focus along the way.

So, having embarked on your open-source journey and actively tackled your first issue, regardless of the outcome, you are a developer! It's time to introduce the critical concept that sets experienced developers apart: the unstuck mindset. This is all about embracing challenges, actively pursuing solutions, and viewing roadblocks as opportunities for growth. Seasoned developers aren't just skilled programmers but experts at getting unstuck. They analyze problems from multiple angles, leveraging their knowledge and resources to find practical and innovative solutions.

Your journey into open source, with its inherent challenges and successes, is the perfect training ground for this critical skill. Whenever you encounter an obstacle, whether deciphering an error message or grappling with unfamiliar code, you actively develop the unstuck mindset. Seeking solutions, using AI assistants, and leveraging online resources demonstrates your growing abilities.

Experiment with different AI assistants! Many offer detailed documentation, helpful tutorials, and sample code to introduce their functionality. Explore how these tools can enhance your workflow and become more proficient. You can find more information about effective AI tool usage on my website[67].

Develop the ability to critically analyze the results provided by AI. While these tools are powerful, they are not always perfect. Learn to interpret AI-generated outputs, identify potential biases, and verify the information with other resources to get a well-rounded perspective.

The world of open source thrives on celebrating small wins. A successful bug fix, a helpful comment in a codebase, or even a thoughtful question to the project community are all achievements to acknowledge and learn from. They fuel your motivation, boost your confidence, and keep you contributing. Getting your first job in software development isn't just about doing one task. You need to keep trying hard and stay involved in the open-source community, where having a good attitude and an open mind is very helpful. You need to contribute again and again.

The learning curve can seem daunting, the open-source landscape is extensive and diverse. But don't let these hurdles deter you. Embrace the unstuck mindset, immerse yourself in the open-source community, and leverage its collaborative spirit. Seek guidance from mentors, and celebrate your progress along the way. With perseverance and a dedication to learning, you will confidently navigate the world of open source, build a strong foundation for your software development career, and reach your goals. The possibilities are truly endless.

---

[67] https://greenlightcareer.tech/book/mindset

PITFALL AVOIDANCE

Y ou've successfully tackled your first open-source challenge
and are gaining serious momentum towards becoming a
software developer. The road ahead is full of learning, but it's also
a long game – requiring dedication and consistent effort, not overnight success. Now, it's time to navigate the common pitfalls that
can derail even the most ambitious coder.

Let's move beyond the idea of overnight success. You might
see others seemingly achieve instant success, but mastering software development requires consistent effort, countless lines of
code, and many bugs squashed along the way, so celebrate your
own milestones – each new skill and each conquered challenge is
a step forward. The learning journey should be viewed as a continuous exploration and evolution rather than a race to the finish
line.

Let's talk about the Imposter Syndrome[68] – that feeling that you
don't truly belong, that you're somehow faking your way through
the software development world. This is a surprisingly common
experience, even among seasoned developers. Focus on your
achievements, no matter how small they seem, and know that

---

[68] https://en.wikipedia.org/wiki/Impostor_syndrome

many others share similar experiences. Employers always want more than you can give. Just accept that you can't know it all. Even after years in software development, I barely scratch the surface of what I need to know.

With its constant highlights of other people's coding successes, social media can sometimes lead to feelings of inadequacy. Resist the urge to compare your journey to others. Everyone's path is unique. Focus on your own progress.

Beware the allure of the new! You're working on your current open-source project when a shiny new programming language or framework catches your eye. It's tempting to abandon your current task and chase the latest fad, like falling into a honeytrap. Resist this urge! Remember your long-term goals. Seeing your current project through, even if it doesn't seem as exciting as the new thing, gives you invaluable experience and builds your credibility within the world of open source.

Life can sometimes get in the way of our pursuits. The initial excitement for learning to code may diminish as other obligations take precedence. This can leave you feeling like your motivation tank is running low. The grind is a natural part of any development journey, and there will be days when coding feels more like a chore than a passion. During these moments, it's essential to reconnect with your core purpose – the driving reasons that inspired you to embark on this adventure. Consider why you chose software development: was it to solve problems, create solutions, or make a positive impact? Understanding your purpose can reignite your inspiration and keep you moving forward. Additionally, revisiting your initial curiosity about coding can remind you of the joy and excitement that sparked your journey in the first place, helping to bridge the gap between your motivation and purpose.

When feeling overwhelmed by the challenges and information overload, take a pit stop. In a classical self-taught approach, abandoning your personal projects when facing challenges can be fatal. However, if you temporarily pause your open-source contributions, the project and its community will continue to thrive without you. They will be ready to welcome you back when you are prepared to re-engage. Taking breaks allows you to recharge, enabling you to return to your contributions with renewed energy and perspective.

Finally, the most valuable learning experiences sometimes come from facing complex issues. So, don't shy away from those quests that initially seem impossible in open-source projects. Embrace the struggle. Use your AI companion, and then write down any new concepts that come to mind. Create a mind map, and don't dive deep into any concept. Remember the idea of thinking about the black box and keeping your tasks in focus. You'll become a more resourceful and well-rounded developer by grappling with complex problems and developing critical thinking.

The road ahead is long, with many opportunities for growth and discovery. Keep your eyes on your long-term goals. With dedication, perseverance, and the ability to learn from any experience, you'll confidently navigate the software development world, ultimately landing your dream job and making your mark in tech.

In the upcoming final book part, we will embark on a transformative journey, bridging the gap between learning to code and successfully completing the main quest of getting hired as a developer. Together, we'll explore effective job-hunting strategies that will equip you with the tools to confidently navigate the competitive job market.

We'll delve into strategies for leveraging your unique strengths and experiences to create a compelling resume that stands out. From identifying your key accomplishments to aligning your skills with the requirements of potential employers, we'll cover every aspect of crafting a persuasive job application. Additionally, we'll provide practical advice on networking, preparing for interviews, and presenting yourself confidently during the hiring process. With each step, we'll empower you to make a lasting impression and increase your chances of securing your dream job.

PART III
Main Quest Speedrun

TIME TO LEVEL UP

Y ou've deftly navigated the neon-lit streets of Software Development City, mastering the art of learning through open-source projects. Like riding an electric scooter from one traffic light to the next, you've transformed challenges into learning opportunities, your skills growing with each issue resolved. Crucially, you've transitioned from passenger to driver, actively shaping your learning journey rather than simply reacting to it. The biggest challenge you face now is demonstrating this transition to potential employers – showing them that you're not just a capable learner but a proactive contributor ready to take the wheel. Now, as you stand at the threshold of the final part of this book, it's time to harness that momentum and venture into the exhilarating world of job hunting.

This chapter introduces the last section of our journey together, where we'll transform your open-source experience into the key that unlocks your dream developer job. The job market is a dynamic arena, and opportunities can disappear in the blink of an eye. It's crucial to act swiftly.

Your contributions to open-source projects are not just lines of code but badges of honor, showcasing your capabilities and dedication. Be ready to weave these experiences into a compelling narrative that will resonate with potential employers.

In the chapters to come, we'll detail how to update your resume with every achievement, turning your job hunt into a thrilling adventure that could lead to a job offer at any moment. We'll explore how to filter job boards with precision, seeking out positions that align perfectly with your now-honed skills.

We will also delve into preparing for job interviews, where your open-source journey will become tales of technical mastery and passion. You'll learn to anticipate common questions and technical challenges, treating them as mini-quests to demonstrate your problem-solving skills.

Networking, too, will be a focus as we'll learn how to form genuine connections within the developer community. These relationships can lead to hidden job opportunities, giving you an edge in the race to secure your dream position.

If you're reading this, you must act now. We've laid the groundwork, providing you with the knowledge and tools you need. You have only a small window to take action before life's distractions pull you away. This is your chance to make a move towards your dream career in software development. Let's embark on this final part of your journey with determination and seize the opportunities that await.

DEPARTMENT OF MOST VALUABLE SKILLS

How do drivers prove their right to drive? They need a driving license. Similarly, we are at a crucial stage in your journey, one that will showcase all the skills you have gained. Think of this stage as visiting a Department of Most Valuable Skills – or DMVS for short. But unlike any government agency, this DMVS is all about you and your unique developer abilities. It's not about a piece of plastic; it's about building your Software Dev License, a.k.a. your resume. In Software Development City, your resume is a living document, constantly evolving as you gain more experience through your open-source contributions.

The beauty of an open-source contributions-based resume is that it goes beyond theoretical knowledge. It's not about showing a list of classes you've attended; it's about demonstrating real-world skills. Your contributions on GitHub are concrete evidence of your abilities, the very skills that employers seek. Imagine a stack of resumes from junior developers who have never worked on a real software project or used version control for team development. Your resume, on the other hand, shows your involvement in genuine projects, with your code publicly available and ready to be reviewed. That difference is what makes you stand out, highlighting your passion for coding.

You might wonder, "How do I start creating this Software Dev License?" Don't worry! The open-source community has your back. There are projects available specifically designed to help you generate a draft resume based on your GitHub activity. These projects will help you organize and present your contributions professionally to potential employers.

One great example is the project at resume.github.com[69]. This repository provides a simple way to create a basic resume based on your public GitHub profile. Simply follow the instructions in the README.md file, star[70] the project, and a resume will be generated at https://resume.github.io/?yourusername. Just make sure your GitHub profile is set to public. For inspiration, you can check out an example like Max Howell's resume (Screenshot 14), showcasing how your repositories and contribution history can highlight your expertise.

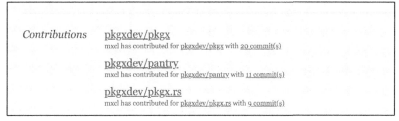

Screenshot 14: Max Howell's contributions in resume.
https://resume.github.io/?mxcl

Another helpful resource is resume-github[71] by Satyem1203. This tool generates a draft resume highlighting your top repositories, statistics, and overall contributions, making it easy to see the scope of your work. What's great is that you don't need to star this

[69] https://github.com/resume/resume.github.com
[70] https://docs.github.com/en/get-started/exploring-projects-on-github/saving-repositories-with-stars
[71] https://github.com/Satyam1203/resume-github

repository to use it. Look at accimeesterlin's example (Screenshot 15) to see how to customize these auto-generated drafts to showcase your unique skills.

Esterling Accime
@accimeesterlin

🖥 | Senior Software Engineer 🎓 | Educator 📖 | Husband

📍 Kennewick, WA

Stats

- 253 Public Repositories
- 36 Following
- 3245 Contributions

- 402 Followers
- 8 Starred repositories

I'm a motivated Github user, for more details about me, visit my Github Profile here.

Screenshot 15: An example of a resume from the "resume-github" project.
https://resume-github.vercel.app/accimeesterlin

In this context, your resume is your badge of honor, a narrative of your path through Software Development City. It's not about the traditional credentials but about showcasing your real-world impact and dedication. In the next chapter, we'll refine this draft into a compelling resume that will unlock doors to your dream developer job. Get ready to let your open-source resume shine and demonstrate your developer prowess to potential employers.

CRAFTING YOUR MASTERPIECE

I n the previous chapter, you took your first steps in creating a draft of your Software Dev License using tools that pull in your open-source contributions. These drafts are a good start, but they are just the foundation. Now, it's time to take ownership and create a resume that will truly grab the attention of hiring managers. You've learned to code, and now you'll learn to market yourself effectively.

Instead of staring at a blank document, wondering where to start, let's leverage the power of the open-source community once again. Head over to the Resume topic[72] on GitHub. You'll discover many projects like Open Resume[73] or resumake.io[74] designed to streamline the resume-building process. However, today, let's focus on a fantastic Reactive-Resume[75] tool by Amruth Pillai. This open-source tool will help you build a functional and genuinely impressive resume. Let's head over to the official Reactive-Resume

---

[72] https://github.com/topics/resume
[73] https://github.com/xitanggg/open-resume
[74] https://github.com/saadq/resumake.io
[75] https://github.com/AmruthPillai/Reactive-Resume

GitHub repository. There, you'll find a wealth of information, including the link to the live, hosted project.

This is what makes Reactive-Resume stand out:

- **OpenAI Integration:** Reactive-Resume integrates with OpenAI, offering suggestions to help you find the best words to describe your skills and accomplishments.

- **Easy Sharing and Customization:** Once you've completed your resume, you can share it via a unique link. Then, you can track views and downloads and customize the page layout for maximum impact.

- **Privacy-Focused:** The Reactive-Resume is designed with user privacy in mind. It does not track your activity or display ads, ensuring your information remains secure.

Upon navigating to the Reactive-Resume website[76] and completing the registration process, you'll be greeted by the main dashboard. Two options present themselves: importing data from an existing LinkedIn profile and building your resume from scratch, both equally valid paths for crafting a stellar resume. You can choose whichever path suits you best. Importing your LinkedIn profile can be a great time-saver, especially if you've already filled out your profile extensively.

We'll be going through the process of building a resume from scratch in this chapter, but feel free to follow along and edit your imported LinkedIn information as we make changes. Click the Create a New Resume section to proceed (Screenshot 16).

The resume editor presents a blank canvas for your masterpiece resume. Don't feel overwhelmed by the fields, icons, and templates. We'll guide you through each section, explaining each element's purpose and how to use it effectively advantage. The left side of the screen is a palette for designing your resume and software development driver's license. Each icon represents a color,

---

[76] https://rxresu.me/

enabling you to choose elements that vividly showcase your skills and experience canvas.

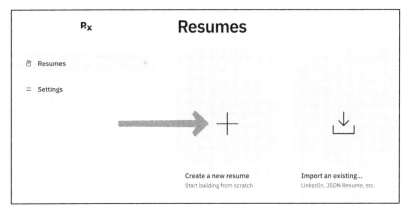

Screenshot 16: Creating a new resume in "Reactive-Resume."
https://rxresu.me/dashboard/resumes

Click the very first Basics icon – the one representing your personal information (Screenshot 17). Upload a photo and a professional headshot to introduce yourself to employers. Next, add your name so it's easy to see. For now, use a placeholder in the Headline section like *"Junior Developer."* You can change this later for each job you apply to.

Now, let's fill in your contact information. Provide your email address, phone number, and location. This section is essential for employers to reach out and invite you to the next stage. Keep it clean and straightforward; we don't need any fancy, unnecessary custom fields.

Next, you'll see a section called Summary. We're actually going to skip that for the moment. Don't worry, we haven't forgotten about it! We'll return to craft a powerful summary that perfectly encapsulates your skills and career goals once we've built out the other sections. Let's just leave that for later.

Next, click on the Profiles icon. This is where you show off your online presence as a software developer. Add at least two key profiles: your LinkedIn profile, which serves as your professional

139

networking hub, and your GitHub profile, showcasing your actual coding work. These profiles are your digital handshake, so make sure they're polished and up to date. Don't worry if you don't have a LinkedIn profile yet. We will create it in the following chapters.

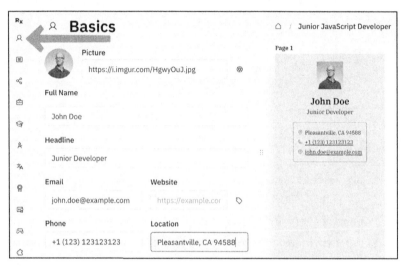

Screenshot 17: Basics section in "Reactive-Resume."

Now let's get into education and certifications. List your educational background, starting with your university and degree. It's okay to include degrees that aren't directly related to tech. They still show that you have valuable skills and are adaptable. When it comes to technical certifications, be selective. Focus on certifications that directly enhance your developer skills and make you a stronger candidate for your target jobs. Avoid non-technical certifications that don't directly contribute to your tech expertise, as they can distract from the core message of your resume.

You've successfully completed the foundational sections of your resume using Reactive-Resume. You're building up your credentials bit by bit. In the next chapter, we will get to the core of your Software Dev License – the Experience section. We'll finally show off your real-world coding experience, and that's where your resume will shine.

HIGHLIGHTING YOUR CONTRIBUTIONS

F inally, we will reveal the secret sauce of the open-source-based resume, marking a crucial moment in your resume-crafting journey. This is where you translate the raw power of your open-source contributions into a compelling narrative for potential employers.

This section of your resume becomes your war chest, overflowing with the spoils you've collected on your open-source quests. Don't worry about grammatical perfection at this stage – focus on capturing the essence of your contributions. We'll finesse the details and polish your prose in future chapters with the help of our trusty AI companion.

Below is a step-by-step guide for building a resume. To keep things simple, I'll choose a random example from resume.github.io, but you should incorporate your own contributions instead. If resume.github.io doesn't work for you for some reason, you can still follow this guide. We use it here solely to summarize the contributions made by users. You are probably familiar with the projects you've contributed to and can remember them without additional tools, right?

Let's peek at the online resume of Chris Wanstrath, co-founder and former CEO of GitHub[77]. His resume will serve as a good example of his open-source contributions, though they are few, much like yours. But don't worry, even a CEO of GitHub might have just a couple of contributions. Go to the Contributions section, featuring Chris's past endeavors. You'll see projects listed with the number of commits he's contributed there. The top line, *"ajaxorg/ace: defunkt has contributed with 5 commit(s),"* readily translates into a resume entry.

Now, let's shift gears and return to the Reactive-Resume builder, where we filled in your contact information in the previous chapter. Here, you have two options for detailing your open-source contributions: the Experience and Projects sections. While both can serve this purpose, there's a subtle difference. Experience entries allow you to specify a location, while Projects showcase a Keywords section. Personally, I advocate for leveraging the Experience section with a location of *Remote* or *GitHub*. This approach allows you to categorize your contributions while keeping a designated Skills section to comprehensively list your technical expertise.

Locate your resume's Experience section and click Add New (Screenshot 18). A window will pop open. In the Company field, enter the name of the project you contributed to. For the Position field, tailor it to the specific language you used (e.g., *JavaScript Developer*). Since this project likely resides in the open-source realm, set the Location to *Remote*.

Let's delve into the example we explored earlier. In Chris Wanstrath's resume draft, the line *"ajaxorg/ace: defunkt has contributed with 5 commit(s)"* contains valuable clues. Notice the presence of multiple links. Click the last one that displays the number of commits (5 in this case). This will lead you to a page

---

[77] https://resume.github.io/?defunkt

142

showcasing Chris's contributions to the ace repository[78]. Like in this example, open the top position link from your resume. Here, you can identify the date of your first and last contributions – valuable details to include in your resume. Copy and paste the link into the Website field in your Reactive-Resume experience entry. There's also a handy label icon on the right-hand side. Click it and create a descriptive label for the link (Screenshot 19), such as *My Commits* or *My Contributions*.

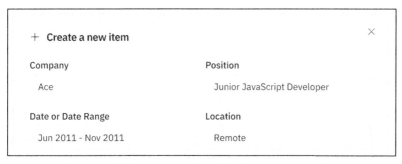

Screenshot 18: An example of the Experience section.

Screenshot 19: Setting the website link label.

The critical moment is here: it's time to summarize your influence on this project. Ideally, each commit you made should have a clear and concise message outlining the changes introduced. Leverage your browser's AI companion to your advantage here. Open the embedded chat or share your screen and prompt the assistant with something like, *"Summarize contributions on the current page, emphasizing the impact of those contributions."* The AI will provide a draft summary based on your commit

---

[78] https://github.com/ajaxorg/ace/commits?author=defunkt

messages (Screenshot 20). This draft becomes your starting point. Adjust and format it appropriately for your resume, removing technical jargon, commit dates, and code samples. Remember, your resume should be professional and free of technical clutter.

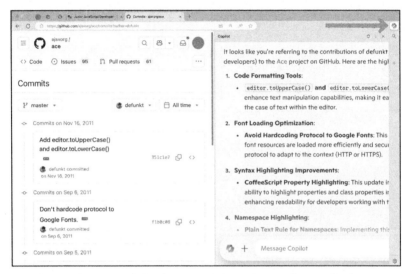

Screenshot 20: MS Copilot summarizing the user's contributions.
https://github.com/ajaxorg/ace/commits?author=defunkt

Remember, your resume should evolve to reflect your growing experience. Each new contribution translates into another brushstroke, enriching the vibrant picture of your skills and dedication. In the following chapter, we'll delve deeper into the world of AI companions, exploring how these powerful tools can further enhance your resume-building process.

LEVERAGE AI BRUSHES

Y ou've successfully navigated the initial stages of crafting your resume using Reactive-Resume. Your open-source contributions are now proudly displayed, each one a testament to your skills and dedication to the software development community. However, the road to a stellar resume continues! This chapter introduces you to advanced techniques rather than new companions or tools.

Reactive-Resume offers multiple options for leveraging the power of AI. The first option involves acquiring an OpenAI API key. This key unlocks various AI functions, enabling you to harness machine learning to enhance your resume. It's like gaining a unique brush that draws itself, providing a wider spectrum of colors and textures for your artistic vision (Screenshot 21). A comprehensive guide on obtaining an OpenAI API key and integrating it with Reactive-Resume can be found in the docs[79].

Another option, however, requires no API key at all. You can utilize ChatGPT[80] as a standalone companion on your resume-building quest. Create your resume in Reactive-Resume and transfer it to ChatGPT for review. This AI helps polish your language

---

[79] https://docs.rxresu.me/product-guides/enabling-openai-integration
[80] https://platform.openai.com/playground/

for a professional and impactful resume. Reactive-Resume guides you in using ChatGPT for a full resume rewrite. Have a look at the detailed guide[81] on using ChatGPT for resume rewriting.

Screenshot 21: Reactive-Resume AI integration capabilities.

Upload your resume as a JSON file to maximize AI chatbot potential. This format helps AI analyze your content for better feedback. A guide on exporting to JSON from Reactive-Resume is in the documentation too[82].

But the AI companions don't stop there! Reactive-Resume also offers a translation prompt[83] specifically designed for use with ChatGPT. This prompt translates your JSON resume into another language, providing a valuable tool for developers pursuing global opportunities.

But remember, AI is here to assist, not replace your creativity.

Now that you know these AI techniques, it's time to revisit the Summary and Skills sections. These sections are often the first seen by HR, so using AI to optimize them can enhance your chances of landing an interview. Fill them out and include Git in your skills; it's essential for a junior developer.

Next chapter, we'll explore resume customization – a crucial tool for every developer heading to Software Development City.

---

[81] https://docs.rxresu.me/product-guides/use-chatgpt-to-rewrite-your-resume

[82] https://docs.rxresu.me/product-guides/exporting-your-resume-as-json

[83] https://docs.rxresu.me/product-guides/translate-your-resume-with-chatgpt

YOUR CUSTOMIZED LOADOUT

Y ou've got your Software Dev License – a solid base resume. Think of it as your character sheet, outlining your core stats and abilities. But in the vast landscape of Software Development City, one loadout won't conquer every quest. Just like a skilled gamer wouldn't tackle a stealth mission with a heavy tank build, you can't approach every job opportunity with the same generic resume. The tech world has many areas to explore, with opportunities spanning front-end, back-end, full-stack, and even mobile development, each with unique challenges and required skill sets.

Within these specializations, even more paths unfold. You could focus on back-end development, but within that, you might find roles using Python with Django, Node.js, or PHP, each requiring a different set of tools and techniques. If you know exactly what type of role you're aiming for – a Python back-end developer with Django, for example – you can definitely craft a resume focusing solely on those technologies. But in the early stages of your career, you might want to cast a wider net and explore your options. Maybe you'd like to try out front-end development or even explore mobile. You must adapt your approach and prepare for different scenarios to do that effectively.

This means creating a resume arsenal – multiple versions of your Software Dev License, each tailored to a specific type of role or technology. Each resume will emphasize projects and skills most relevant to a specific job description. Think of it as choosing the right tool for the job. When applying for a front-end position, emphasize your UI skills and JavaScript proficiency. When going for a back-end role in Node.js, you'd highlight your experience with that environment. Each position requires a specialized approach, and you must be ready.

Determining precisely what keywords to highlight for each position can be challenging. While you know your own skills from your open-source contributions, you need to align them with each employer's specific needs. Fortunately, AI can be your ally in this. By feeding your initial resume and a job posting to an AI tool, you can identify how to best match your skill set to the job requirements. This way, you can make sure to highlight the most relevant aspects of your skills and background for each role you are applying for.

Of course, we'd all like to get the dream job immediately. But life sometimes throws curveballs. You might need to take a tech-related position that's not exactly where you initially planned to go just to gain more experience and build a strong foundation for the future. It's essential to be open to different opportunities and not limit yourself to a narrow set of targets. This way, your search is more flexible, and you're more likely to get your foot in the door.

In the next chapter, we will explore the diverse world of opportunities available in Software Development City. We'll compare different paths to success, such as freelancing, full-time employment, and contract positions. We'll explore the pros and cons of each path so you can choose which direction you want to take on your road to a fulfilling career.

PATHWAYS TO COMPLETING THE MAIN QUEST

You've crafted your customized resumes, your Software Dev License is ready, and you've even learned how to adapt it for different types of opportunities. Now it's time to decide: what adventure awaits you? Many paths lead forward, and your main quest may vary depending on your choice.

Let's look at your options. You could try freelancing, where you choose your own projects and clients. It's exciting to be your own boss, set your own hours, and manage your work. But freelancing has its downsides. You'll always need to find new clients, face unpredictable income, and market yourself. Be prepared for extra work – weekends may be busy too.

Then, there are the towering skyscrapers of contract work, offering high-stakes missions and higher pay. Contract positions are like mercenary gigs – you join a team for a specific project and then move on. The financial rewards might be appealing, but the assignments are temporary, and you'll need to constantly seek new opportunities, especially when the economy is down.

The neon lights of entrepreneurship also flicker on the horizon, promising untold riches and creative freedom. Gurus on YouTube often paint a picture of effortlessly creating startups, becoming millionaires, getting a waifu, living in Bali, and spending all day surfing. But if you look closer, you'll often see that their revenue comes from selling programming courses or tech stacks to people like you. So be aware that you might be the product in that equation.

Software Development City offers various paths. You could become a storyteller in the Content Creation area by sharing knowledge through blog posts, tutorials, or videos – no need to be a guru, just document your journey. This can also generate income.

In the Teaching and Mentoring area, you can guide aspiring developers and share your knowledge. Just ensure you level up first before teaching others.

Consider Bug Bounty programs for an ethical way to earn money by finding software vulnerabilities. This option is best for experienced developers who can identify and report security flaws, helping make the internet safer while getting paid. If you enjoy problem-solving, Competitive Programming offers another way to earn money through contests, but it also requires strong coding skills and experience to succeed.

So, as you can see, there are many ways to win in Software Development City. Each path offers a unique experience and set of challenges. However, to begin your main quest, a solid foundation is key. That's why we'll focus on full-time employment for the next part of our journey together. A full-time job can provide stability, mentorship, and a clear path for career growth. It's a solid base for further exploration of the other paths and opportunities later in your career. In the coming chapters, we will delve into the process of securing a full-time position, equipping you with the strategies needed to navigate the job market and ace those interviews. This is the first step in making your dreams a reality.

BUILDING YOUR CAREER FOUNDATION

S oftware Development City pulses with energy, and the idea of securing a full-time position feels like finding a safe haven in this dynamic environment. You hold your resume and hard-earned Software Dev License, knowing it represents a path towards more than just a salary. You're drawn to the idea of a development team working together towards a common goal and experienced mentors who can guide your progress.

Permanent roles, you see, are like training camps for aspiring developers. They offer a structured environment where you can gain knowledge, learn new technologies, and be guided by experienced professionals. You'll have the opportunity to hone your skills and work on projects with the latest tech, all while receiving guidance from veterans in the field.

The advantages of full-time employment extend beyond skill-building and access to resources. It offers financial security and a steady income that allows you to focus on your growth and not just make ends meet. Benefits such as health insurance, paid time off, and even the possibility of a retirement plan add to the sense of stability and security.

While the freedom of freelancing and contract work might still tempt you, you recognize the value of laying a strong foundation first. You're not yet prepared to navigate the unpredictable nature of the gig economy by yourself. A permanent position provides the learning and experience you need to eventually thrive independently.

You're also aware of the possible challenges of full-time positions. Not every team will be a perfect fit, and not every project will be successful. The learning curve in software development can be steep, and there will be moments when you encounter challenges. You might face bugs that seem impossible to fix or deadlines that feel unachievable, and you'll need to deal with constant pressure from management, forcing you to adapt and learn quickly.

Even if your first position doesn't work out perfectly, the experience you gain is still invaluable. It won't only be the knowledge you will obtain but also your resume, which won't be empty anymore. This commercial development experience will make you more attractive to potential employers as you apply for new positions in the future. This also will equip you with the soft skills that will help you navigate the world of software development.

As you prepare to enter the job market, you have a clear goal in mind. In the next chapter, we'll explore where you can find these full-time opportunities and start your journey toward your first professional software development role. Get ready to explore the next level of your trip.

NAVIGATING RECRUITMENT OUTPOSTS

I n the previous chapter, we explored the benefits and challenges of a full-time position in Software Development City. Now, it's time to learn where to find those opportunities. Think of job boards as bustling recruitment outposts scattered throughout the city. You might remember visiting these places early in your journey – back then, they felt like chaotic, overwhelming places with no clear way to get a job. You also might have thought that the system was rigged against you. But now, armed with your open-source contributions and a strong resume, you're ready to confidently approach them. Your Software Dev License now shows your proven skills, and even if you're not a level 70 developer, your resume now has some real-world experience.

So, what exactly are job boards, and how do they function? They are places where companies post announcements for open positions detailing the skills and experience they need, much like posting wanted posters in a town square. They come in various types. General job boards, like Totaljobs[84], attract many employers

---

[84] https://www.totaljobs.com/

and job seekers. Industry-specific boards cater to professionals with particular skill sets, like Dice[85] or eFinancialCareers[86]. And niche boards like Climatebase[87], where companies focus on specific areas and post their needs.

To navigate these job board outposts effectively, you must know which ones are most relevant to your developer journey. This landscape varies depending on your location. Just like different areas of Software Development City require specialized maps, you'll need to identify the job boards most popular in your country or region. Ask for advice from your fellow developers in online communities and forums. They can point you to the most frequented recruitment outposts for the roles you seek. It's all about targeting the right places to maximize your chances of success.

Be mindful, though, as not all outposts are trustworthy. Like any bustling city, job boards can attract some unscrupulous individuals. Be wary of offers that sound too good to be true, and never pay fees upfront for a job application. Legitimate job boards connect you with employers for free. Trust your instincts and avoid any suspicious-looking offers.

It's also important to understand that job boards are not the only way to connect with potential employers. While they are helpful, they might not be the most direct path to HR contacts within specific companies. But don't worry. We'll explore other strategies to expand your reach and discover hidden opportunities in the chapters ahead. In the next chapter, we'll dive into a practical example and learn how to use job boards to search effectively, equipping you with the skills to navigate these bustling outposts and identify the perfect opportunities for your developer journey.

---

[85] https://www.dice.com/
[86] https://www.efinancialcareers.co.uk/
[87] https://climatebase.org/

CONQUERING THE OUTPOST

Welcome back! You've explored the different types of job board outposts. Now, let's focus on mastering one of the largest: Indeed (Screenshot 22). Think of Indeed as a sprawling, multi-level skyscraper packed with potential opportunities for software developers like you.

Screenshot 22: One of the biggest job boards – "Indeed".
https://indeed.com/

To navigate Indeed effectively, you need a clear vision of your ideal role. Start by defining your desired job title, industry, and location. Indeed's search[88] function is your tool to pinpoint your perfect role. Don't be afraid to try different search terms – use

---

[88] https://www.indeed.com/career-advice/finding-a-job/tips-on-how-to-get-better-search-results-on-indeed.com

synonyms and related fields to broaden your search and discover hidden opportunities.

Remember those keywords we discussed earlier? Indeed's search engine works similarly. Incorporate relevant keywords and industry-specific terms into your search queries to attract the most relevant job postings. Start with the technologies you've used during your open-source contributions. It's a great way to leverage your existing experience.

Having defined your search parameters and used effective keywords, it's time to master Indeed's filters (Screenshot 23). These filters are like specialized tools that enhance your ability to navigate the bustling recruitment center. Indeed offers various filters – job type, salary expectations, experience level, date posted, and company size. These helps refine your search results and focus on the most relevant opportunities.

Screenshot 23: Image showcasing the "Indeed" search filters.

Having narrowed your search results, don't be too strict with the location filter. Indeed allows you to explore opportunities beyond your immediate area, potentially uncovering exciting remote work possibilities. The world of software development is not limited by geography, so consider casting a wider net in your search.

Job postings don't always disappear the moment they're filled. While it's good practice to prioritize new listings, don't disregard older ones. Some companies take longer to fill roles. Your well-crafted application could be the key to unlocking that opportunity. Another thing to be aware of is the existence of bait job postings, particularly during economic downturns. Some recruitment agencies post fake opportunities to build a talent pool for future use, so be ready for potentially useless conversations.

Once you've found promising opportunities, use Indeed's sorting and saving features to prioritize your leads. Sort your results by relevance or date posted. The Save function is your bookmark, allowing you to keep track of interesting opportunities you want to revisit later (Screenshot 24).

Screenshot 24: An example of an "Indeed" job posting.

But your journey doesn't stop with just identifying potential roles. Indeed offers company pages, giving you a basic understanding of each company. Use this information and some additional Google or AI research to tailor your resume and cover letter. Focus on the specific skills and experiences relevant to each employer, increasing your chances of landing an interview.

After conducting a search and refining your results, look for the Job Alert option[89] to set up email notifications for new matching roles. However, be careful not to overwhelm yourself with emails. You can adjust the frequency of job alerts and select daily, weekly, or less frequent updates.

Now that you've learned to use Indeed, you're better equipped to navigate the recruitment outposts across Software Development City. In the next chapter, we'll delve deeper into the world of HR professionals. Who are they, and what are they looking for? Let's find out in the next chapter.

---

[89] https://support.indeed.com/hc/en-gb/articles/204488890

UNDERSTANDING THE GATEKEEPERS

You've conquered Indeed – the most significant job board outpost. Now it's time to face the gatekeepers who guard the path to your dream software development role: HR professionals and recruiters. Understanding their roles and motivations is crucial for navigating the recruitment process successfully.

In Software Development City, HR departments act as the gatekeepers, deciding who gets to join or leave the digital battlefield. You'll usually encounter HR twice: first, when they welcome you with promises of great adventures, and later, when they might politely escort you out. So, always treat them with respect. But don't let that interaction get too emotional.

However, our focus today is on recruiters, sometimes called Talent Acquisition Specialists. Consider them scouts venturing outside city walls to find talented adventurers for their companies. Recruiters collaborate with HR to clarify job requirements and seek candidates through job boards, social media, professional networks, and personal databases of contacts.

Beyond the initial sourcing, recruiters manage the interview process, facilitating communication between candidates, hiring managers, and teams, sometimes even negotiating offers.

Recruiters are the first line in recruitment, using resume screening as a filter to identify candidates with required skills and experience. Though some filters are automated, many conduct manual assessments. Given the large volume of applications, clearly and concisely presenting your skills is essential crucial.

The resume screening process often acts as a non-technical filter, risking the exclusion of talented individuals without traditional computer science degrees. Companies may outsource recruitment to agencies that prioritize speed over understanding the role. In these cases, the focus might be on simply getting a warm body in the seat. This doesn't mean you should avoid positions managed by recruitment agencies. However, you should understand their motivations and tailor your approach accordingly.

These recruiters are headhunters seeking valuable talent, and you are the prey they're pursuing. Companies hire them to track down the best candidates, paying bounties for successful placements. So make yourself a worthwhile target – showcase your skills prominently and respond quickly. The best opportunities go to those who get noticed first and prove their worth.

Even if you pass the initial screening and get an interview but are unsuccessful, you can still help the recruiter. Be prepared to explain the task and what the interviewer asked you in detail. This will help them fill the position with another candidate. Why is this important? Because they will remember you and most likely send you to the next opportunity. Even if they don't hire you now, you will at least provide them with valuable insight into the employer's interview process, increasing your chances in the future.

While recruiters are traditional gatekeepers in Software Development City, networking with fellow developers can uncover hidden paths to your dream companies. Strategic networking can reveal opportunities and occasionally bypass gatekeepers.

PICKING LOCKS

With the chatter of job boards behind you, you've learned about the gatekeepers of HR and recruiters. Now, it's time to delve into the heart of Software Development City, where the real treasures lie hidden. Here, networking acts as your secret passage, allowing you to connect directly with developers and professionals, bypassing some traditional recruitment obstacles.

Networking is like a network of hidden pathways that weave through the city, offering access to opportunities not visible at first glance. While maintaining a good relationship with recruiters is beneficial, networking is your stealthy approach, akin to a rogue finding backdoor in a fortress. It's a social dance, a series of introductions and conversations that can seem daunting, especially if you're more at home with code than crowds.

However, keep in mind that even the most introverted adventurers thrive by forming connections. Technical prowess is your sword, but networking is your picklock, opening doors that might otherwise stay locked. Embracing this skill can unlock your full potential in this bustling city.

Developers value real-world contributions over resumes stuffed with keywords. This is where meetups shine as bustling taverns where you can exchange tales of your coding adventures.

You showcase your passion and dedication by sharing your GitHub projects, even if they're still evolving. These gatherings are not just social events; they're networking goldmines. By engaging in discussions, you can attract the attention of established developers, scouting for new team members. So, hone your social skills, prepare to talk about your projects, and immerse yourself in these community events.

The power of a reference is like discovering a hidden passage into a fortress. A strong recommendation from someone within your target company can be your golden ticket, bypassing traditional HR gatekeepers. A reference from a trusted colleague is a glowing endorsement of your skills and potential. How do you get such endorsements? Through networking. Building relationships with developers in your target companies increases your chances of securing that crucial reference.

While meetups offer a casual networking environment, job fairs are another setting where you can connect. Imagine them as vibrant marketplaces where you can interact directly with potential employers. Here, you can demonstrate your coding abilities and interpersonal skills, showing you're a competent developer and a great team player. This face-to-face interaction can significantly boost your visibility in the industry.

In the upcoming chapter, we will shift our focus to online networking, a vital complement to your physical networking efforts. The digital landscape is rich with platforms where developers gather, share, and connect. By leveraging these spaces, you can expand your network, reach those inaccessible through traditional means, and gain industry insights. Whether you're looking for mentorship, advice, or job opportunities, online networking can be transformative in your journey to becoming a recognized member of the software development community. Prepare for a virtual adventure as we explore how to effectively network online in the next chapter.

THE UNTAMED ONLINE WILDERNESS

You've learned the power of in-person networking in Software Development City but might also be hesitant. After all, venturing into bustling meetups and job fairs can be daunting. Luckily, the digital world offers a vast, online wilderness filled with opportunities to connect with fellow developers and potential employers from the comfort of your own space.

A strong online presence is vital for networking. Focus on a niche in software development that interests you, like web or game development. This will help you build a targeted persona, attracting like-minded connections. Use your specialty to engage with other developers online.

Where to start this journey? Begin with the well-known trails of general software development subreddits like r/learnprogramming[90], r/cscareerquestions[91], r/ExperiencedDevs[92], r/webdev[93], and

---

[90] https://www.reddit.com/r/learnprogramming/
[91] https://www.reddit.com/r/cscareerquestions/
[92] https://www.reddit.com/r/ExperiencedDevs/
[93] https://www.reddit.com/r/webdev/

r/gamedev[94], where all sorts of developers gather. Engage in discussions, ask questions, and share knowledge to demonstrate your passion and expertise. You can also seek out programming buddies (Screenshot 25) who might enhance your skills or broaden your network. Remember, involvement in these communities can forge lasting connections.

r/django · 1 yr. ago

I am looking for a pair programming coding buddy as I am working on my first django project django delights.

We can do it online or remote. For those looking for collaboration experience and portfolio project work. this is really for project experience and a partner to program with. I am not looking to pay to have someone build a website for me but more for someone else that is looking to build a portfolio to get a resume and get a django job.

Message me your availability.

Screenshot 25: A Reddit user seeks programming buddies.
https://www.reddit.com/r/django/comments/17dc6ja/

Remember that feeling of uncertainty you experienced at the train station at the beginning of your adventure? Believe it or not, this is a common feeling for new developers. You might see posts like *"I learned nothing from my CS Degree. What now?"* on r/cscareerquestions (Screenshot 26). This is why online communities are so valuable: they offer a space to share your challenges, learn from others, and build connections based on shared experiences.

In fact, this was the first post I encountered on the r/cscareerquestions subreddit, and it opened my eyes to how many aspiring developers feel lost about their next steps. That's why I decided to write this book – to guide and support you on your software development journey, helping you navigate challenges and unlock your potential.

---

[94] https://www.reddit.com/r/gamedev/

After exploring general subreddits, delve into tech stack-specific ones like r/Python[95] or r/reactjs[96]. These communities focus on developers using particular technologies and will connect you with peers who share your expertise.

Screenshot 26: A Reddit user's frustration.
https://www.reddit.com/r/cscareerquestions/comments/1catejd/

Beyond subreddits, explore Discord servers and vibrant online oases for specific programming languages or frameworks. Discord servers, like the Python server[97] or the Java server[98], boast tens of thousands of members, offering a treasure trove of connections. You will find lasting connections if you learn how to navigate these bustling communities.

Be aware of the bottomless swamps that exist in the form of social media platforms like X (formerly Twitter). These platforms can be time-consuming distractions, offering little in the way of meaningful connections. While some interaction on these platforms is okay, focus on building relationships to help you achieve your goals rather than just consuming content.

So, how do you move from a passive lurker to a valued member of these communities? Be engaged. Participate in discussions,

---

[95] https://www.reddit.com/r/Python/
[96] https://www.reddit.com/r/reactjs/
[97] https://discord.com/invite/python
[98] https://discord.com/invite/together-java-272761734820003841

ask good questions, and offer insights. Don't be afraid to look stupid. You've come a long way, and everything has a reason. Every path starts with those first steps. Remember that the goal is to learn, share your knowledge, and make connections. Consistent participation helps establish your presence within the community.

Now that you're equipped with the basics of survival let's delve deeper into the art of forging connections within the online wilderness. Focus your outreach strategically. Connect with junior developers who recently landed their dream jobs for valuable insights and seek mentorship from experienced developers in your niche. Personalize your outreach to developers by showing genuine interest in their work. Reference their projects, and instead of asking for a job, suggest a brief 15-minute coffee chat to learn from their experiences. Many developers appreciate sharing knowledge and enjoy feeling valued.

Finally, remember the connections you've already made during your open-source contributions. Many project maintainers list contact information on their profiles. Use the trust you've built by contributing to their projects and ask for a virtual coffee chat. Discuss your career goals, seek advice, or ask about potential referrals.

The online wilderness may seem vast, but with the right skills, you can navigate digital landscapes and forge connections. Consider joining our community[99], where readers share experiences and support each other another. Check out my website for more information and to join us. The next chapter will demonstrate how online communities empower members to succeed. It will provide an example of a community's best practices, serving as a guide for your journey.

---

[99] https://greenlightcareer.tech/book/community

THE POWER OF PURPOSE-DRIVEN COMMUNITIES

Y our journey through the online wilderness has given you the skills to explore its depths. But simply exploring isn't the final goal. As a developer, you have the potential to impact the world, and connecting with like-minded individuals is a powerful way to achieve it. So, let's take a closer look at one online community, ClimateAction.Tech[100] (CAT), and see how it fosters collaboration and purpose.

Imagine a dense, vibrant rainforest within this wilderness, full of life. This is ClimateAction.Tech community where tech professionals unite to tackle the climate crisis. It's a crucial ecosystem where innovation thrives and real-world impact takes shape. If your coding explorations have involved climate-focused GitHub projects, then ClimateAction.Tech is a great place to connect and learn.

This community of developers is driven by a powerful shared purpose: to make climate action[101] a top priority within the tech industry. They believe in taking responsibility for technology's

---

[100] https://climateaction.tech/
[101] https://climateaction.tech/actions/

environmental impact, working towards a future where the tech industry champions sustainability. This shared vision provides the community a strong foundation, uniting its members to build a better future.

ClimateAction.Tech's beauty lies in its inclusive nature, much like the biodiversity of a rainforest. It's a vibrant community[102] with over 10,000 members from across the globe, a diverse mix of skill levels and backgrounds. In this rainforest of code, seasoned developers collaborate with those just starting to bloom. Whether you are a coding veteran or new to this quest, your perspective is valuable within this community. ClimateAction.Tech welcomes everyone who shares a passion for a more sustainable future (Screenshot 27).

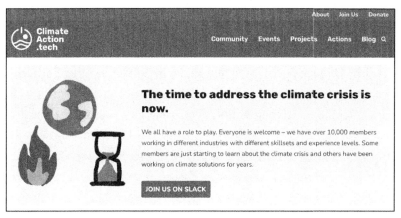

Screenshot 27: ClimateAction.Tech website.
https://climateaction.tech/

Instead of grand pronouncements, the community's activities are focused on real-world actions (Screenshot 28), and you will be part of them. Every activity serves as a firm root in fertile ground, helping businesses transform their processes through the integration of sustainability. The community assists developers in creating eco-friendly applications by providing the necessary skills.

---

[102] https://climateaction.tech/community/

Additionally, there is an advocacy for including sustainable practices during the early stages of product design and promoting green and low-carbon solutions.

Business Culture & Behavior Change	Green Software Engineering	Sustainable Product Design	Low-Carbon Infrastructure
We want businesses to prioritize climate issues and embed sustainability requirements into the day-to-day work of all employees.	Software engineers can make decisions which reduce the carbon pollution of their applications.	We can change the product design process to reduce upstream and downstream emissions.	While we transition to renewable energy, we can align compute load with low-carbon energy.

Screenshot 28: Pillars of the ClimateAction.Tech community.

ClimateAction.Tech emphasizes collective engagement in action. The community thrives on various initiatives, each playing a role in the ecosystem. Imagine these initiatives as vital gathering places within the rainforest. For example, to help onboarding the new members, ClimateAction.Tech provides a simple checklist. You will set aside 15-30 minutes to get to know the community and read all relevant materials. There's a direct Slack channel connection with other members to ensure help will come whenever needed. ClimateAction.Tech also sponsors members through CAT Mini-Grants[103] or regular meetings with a fellow member using the #cat-roulette[104] Slack channel and the weekly newsletter[105] of handpicked articles and event updates. Another helpful place to learn is through CAT Knowledge Base[106] or Branch Magazine[107],

---

[103] https://climateaction.tech/projects/cat-mini-grants/
[104] https://climateaction.tech/projects/cat-roulette/
[105] https://buttondown.com/climateActionTech/
[106] https://climateaction.tech/blog/meet-the-cat-knowledge-base-a-resource-that-supports-community-learning-and-action/
[107] https://climateaction.tech/projects/branch-magazine/

where everyone shares their solutions and thoughts on sustainable internet and beyond.

ClimateAction.Tech provides opportunities for continuous skill growth and expands knowledge of climate-related technologies. Within its digital boundaries, this community acts as a space for growth, cultivating your abilities and improving your understanding of climate challenges. You are developing your needed skills by actively participating in discussions and working with fellow members. Do not be afraid to ask for assistance from more experienced members. This collective sharing and support can be found within their Slack channel.

More and more companies value sustainability, actively seeking developers who are passionate about creating a greener future. But how can you connect with those that share those ideals? ClimateAction.Tech acts like a hidden connection within the digital landscape. Within their Slack channel and newsletter, companies often post opportunities closely aligned with the values of ClimateAction.Tech. By actively participating, demonstrating your expertise through projects by working with open-source software, and engaging with the community, you're increasing visibility with companies that value your skillset and the sustainability principles you believe in.

As a developer, you may experience moments of doubt, and at times, the digital journey can feel isolating, leading to feelings of climate anxiety. But ClimateAction.Tech offers refuge from these solitary moments, just like a place where you will feel warm while exploring the rainforest on your own.

ClimateAction.Tech offers a helping hand to those eager to make a difference. This welcoming community offers mentors, peers, and abundant resources to help you grow. So, join[108] the cause, put your skills to good use, and explore the vast potential of technology for positive change.

---

[108] https://climateaction.tech/actions/join-a-community/

MULTIPASS TO OPPORTUNITY

The echoing calls of exotic birds fade as you transition back to the city, arriving at LinkedIn, the bustling terminal of Software Development City. Here, everyone is in their formal professional attire, unlike the free-flowing online wilderness. This grand airport hums with the energy of countless possibilities. Your resume – your digital driving license has carried you thus far. Now, you need a new document – a developer's passport – to access the most promising opportunities in this digital metropolis.

Before you stretch, a vast departures and arrivals board will display job openings ranging from startups to established tech corporations. Each listing represents a potential flight toward a new team, project, or challenge. However, boarding those flights requires passing through the discerning eyes of recruiters, the gatekeepers of this world. They carefully examine each traveler to verify they possess the right skills and background for their desired destination.

Your LinkedIn profile acts as your passport and identity document. It is your chance to present your skills and experience in a manner that captures the attention of those holding the keys to your desired employment.

Crafting a compelling headline is like having your passport photo taken, your first impression. It must grab attention. Your headline must be a brief and impressive synopsis of your coding experience.

Just as a well-used passport contains stamps and visas from exotic locations, your LinkedIn profile should testify to your adventures as a developer. Your contributions to open-source projects testify to your digital adventures across the code landscape.

You have a couple of options for showcasing your open-source involvement. The first is in the Experience section, similar to displaying previous places of work. Still, open-source contributions can work very well since you don't have commercial experience. Were you the project lead? Did you debug a critical bug? These are experiences to highlight.

Another place to display your accomplishments is the Project section, which can be like a photo album of digital adventures. Here, you can display all your projects, including short descriptions with links to repositories. Highlight specific actions taken within each, like fixing code, adding features, or creating excellent documentation.

Remember that the recruiters need hard evidence of your expertise. If you can measure your impact from these actions, be sure to note them in your profile. Did a particular bug fix create user interaction or engagement? Was a function made efficient enough that it decreased computational effort? These kinds of details will make your profile stand out.

As you shape your LinkedIn profile, add skills within descriptions and headline so the correct searches can recognize it and connect you with appropriate job offers.

The journey to your career aspirations can be full of twists and turns, but having a professional profile will help you take a huge step forward.

NAVIGATING THE
TERMINAL

W ith your passport now gleaming with your skills and experience, it's time to delve deeper into the bustling terminal of LinkedIn, a dynamic hub filled with thousands of job opportunities. Consider the Jobs tab on LinkedIn as a flight board, constantly updating with software development opportunities. It offers more choices, numerous remote jobs, and the convenience of borderless employment through an Easy Apply feature, unlike Indeed or other job boards.

Imagine being at an airport, searching the flight board for your flight. LinkedIn offers thousands of job opportunities instead of just a few flights. That's why proper filters are crucial for finding what you need.

LinkedIn's search tools (Screenshot 29) are your digital filters, helping you find opportunities aligned with your career path. Use these filters[109] to refine your search by location, job title, and technologies. Company size can also be relevant. These tools act like

---

[109] https://www.linkedin.com/help/linkedin/answer/a524335

airport control panels, guiding you through options to find the best match for your developer skills.

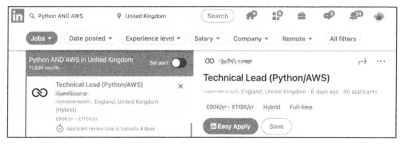

Screenshot 29: LinkedIn job search example.
https://www.linkedin.com/jobs/search/?keywords=Python
%20AND%20AWS

Once you've identified a promising opportunity, it's time to prepare for your application. Remember your resume – your developer's driving license? While a general resume might pass initial screenings, a tailored resume and cover letter are crucial for securing an interview. When applying through LinkedIn, you can attach your resume. Tailor your application to each type of job description. Soon, you'll start recognizing patterns and job types, noting which technologies are often used together.

Of course, the ideal scenario is writing a unique cover letter for each application, but this isn't always mandatory. As you recognize these patterns, prepare cover letters and resumes for different job types and tech stacks. Highlight how your skills and experience directly match the job requirements. Quantify your relevant achievements to show the value you can add to the team. Remember, it's a numbers game. Your task is to learn how to apply quickly but accurately – don't send a Python-focused resume to a front-end developer role; avoid such mismatches.

No pilot embarks on a solo flight – they rely on a network of air traffic controllers, ground crew, and fellow pilots for a safe and successful journey. Similarly, navigating the vast LinkedIn terminal requires a robust network of connections. Remember the wilderness of online networking? The connections you build on LinkedIn function as your support crew in this new environment.

- **Seek Out Your Wingmen:** While a robust network is valuable, starting small is okay. Begin by connecting with classmates, professors, and past colleagues. Their endorsements and recommendations are pre-flight checks, vouching for your skills and experience.

- **Informational Interviews:** Reach out to professionals in your desired field for informational interviews. These conversations are valuable reconnaissance missions, providing insights into specific companies, roles, and industry trends.

- **Target Your Talent Acquisition Specialists:** Don't forget recruiters who guide developers to exciting opportunities. Connect with them in your target location, expressing interest in relevant positions. Be concise in your message and emphasize your openness to new opportunities.

- **Endorsements and Recommendations:** As discussed, connection endorsements act as visa stamps on your developer passport, building your credibility. Endorse your connections' skills and politely request recommendations to further solidify your qualifications.

- **Expanding Your Circle:** With a limited network initially, consider connecting with second-degree connections (Screenshot 30) – connections of your connections. Use LinkedIn filters to strategically grow your network. Consistency is crucial; repeat this process periodically to build a strong network supporting your developer journey.

The Jobs tab offers opportunities, but don't underestimate direct networking as discussed in previous chapters. Consider developers at your target companies to be fellow adventurers who've reached success in Software Development. Connect with them for advice or referrals. While developers' shyness may lower response rates, a good connection can yield invaluable insights and opportunities that job boards may overlook.

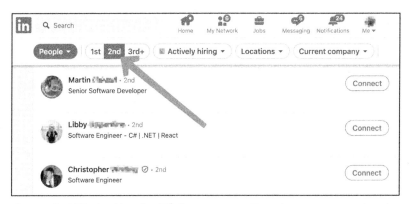

Screenshot 30: Looking for 2nd-degree connections to grow your network.
https://www.linkedin.com/search/results/people/?network
=%5B%22S%22%5D

Share your achievements confidently! Update your LinkedIn with project milestones, new features from open-source contributions, or challenges overcome. These posts serve as digital networking tools that can create new opportunities and advance your career.

Continuously update and refine your profile to showcase your skills, experience, and achievements. Use keywords relevant to your field and aspirations. Consider seeking feedback from peers or mentors to enhance your profile's effectiveness.

The job search can be daunting, and many fear rejection, which may stop them from applying or interviewing. Like the fear of flying, the fear of rejection can be managed through understanding. Just as knowledge can ease the fear of flight, knowing rejection is common can alleviate anxiety. Everyone faces rejection – it doesn't define your worth or your job-seeking abilities.

Face the fear of rejection gradually. Like exposure therapy for flying, applying for jobs you're unsure about helps you become comfortable with rejection. The more you encounter it, the easier it becomes.

Rejection isn't the end. A fear of flying doesn't stop you from flying, and fear of rejection won't prevent you from getting a job. Don't let rejection discourage you; instead, learn from it. Every "no" brings you closer to a "yes."

As you start your job search, remember it's a journey, not a sprint. Challenges will arise, but with patience and optimism, you'll reach your destination. Confront your anxieties to pursue your dream job. You've navigated digital terrains; this is just another chapter.

The next chapter explores the game rules and complications that will transform our safe journey through Software Development City into a gladiator arena. As money enters the equation, our tranquil city will become a treacherous landscape of challenges. Your camaraderie and skills will be tested in a realm where reputation is currency and every decision counts. Prepare for a thrilling journey with high stakes, fierce competition, and a razor-thin line between success and failure. Are you ready to step into the arena?

YOUR TICKET TO
COLISEUM

The echoing chatter of the LinkedIn terminal fades as you board a sleek, high-speed aircraft. Your developer passport gleams, your network is established, and your resume – your developer's driving license – is polished to perfection. Do you remember the thrill of navigating the sprawling city of software development on your trusty scooter, where your technical abilities evolved through the challenges posed by traffic lights? The job hunt is a different beast – a fierce battleground that demands different skills.

Don't let the polished facade of the LinkedIn airport terminal confuse you – it's not a calm flight where everything goes according to plan. You can't expect a smooth journey – there will be turbulence, delays, and unexpected challenges. Your boarding pass and application are your ticket to the gladiatorial arena, where mortal combat begins. Politics, biases, and a fair bit of luck can be involved. This is no longer a playground; it's a coliseum where warriors fight for glory, and only the most resilient emerge victorious. Today marks the beginning of the most crucial stage in the main quest to secure your dream job within the sprawling city. Here, your technical skills remain a formidable weapon, but mastering the soft skills of the job hunt arena will ultimately determine your success.

Imagine yourself as a gladiator entering the arena, competing for the same prize as many others. This is the reality of each job application. Recruiters, like gatekeepers, receive hundreds of applications for one position. They sift through mountains of documents, seeking potential champions. Just as a gladiator doesn't expect personal attention from the crowd, don't expect detailed feedback from every recruiter. They aim to quickly identify candidates who closely match the perfect fit for the role, aligning skills and experience with the job description.

Think back to how you managed in the wilderness by being resourceful and making your own way. Job hunting is a bit like that; you need to rely on yourself. Recruiters can help by finding you opportunities, but remember, they are focused on filling jobs quickly. This means they might not have time to understand what makes you unique. To take charge of your job search, you must be proactive and determined.

In the gladiator arena, a skilled warrior knows which battles to prioritize. Similarly, navigating the job hunt requires strategic filtering and prioritizing of opportunities. Focus your energy on the positions that align most closely with your career goals and skill set.

Think about the gladiatorial pit: constant chasing can lead to tiredness and weakness. Likewise, sending too many follow-up emails to recruiters is usually not needed; if they see potential in you, they'll get in touch. Too many reminders can come off as pushy or desperate. Save your energy for important tasks: apply for new jobs, write strong applications, and get ready for interviews. That's where your true fighting spirit shines. In the next chapter, we'll look at a full job search plan and daily routine, a strategy that will give you the key skills to succeed in your job search and land your dream role in Software Development.

In the next chapter, we'll delve into a comprehensive job search plan and daily routine, a battle plan that will equip you with the essential strategies and tactics to conquer the job hunt arena and secure your dream position within the city of software development.

THE WARRIOR'S ROUTINE

T he daily grind of the job search process resembles the gladiator arena season, where preparation is paramount. Like
gladiators train relentlessly, job seekers dedicate countless hours
to scouring job boards, polishing resumes, and refining interview
techniques. This daily grind is the rigorous training that prepares
them for the intense job market competition. Networking becomes a strategic maneuver, forging alliances and connections like
gladiators building camaraderie. Through this relentless pursuit,
job seekers transform into formidable contenders, ready to face
the challenges of the job search arena and emerge triumphant.

Imagine yourself as a seasoned warrior, honing your skills each
morning in preparation for the day's battle: job interviews. A
structured job search schedule is your training regimen, ensuring
you dedicate focused time to each crucial task. Think of your cal-
endar app as your quest log, meticulously detailing the activities
planned for each day. Juggling multiple responsibilities is inevita-
ble – consider this the art of wielding several weapons simultane-
ously. The key lies in effective time management, ensuring each
activity receives the necessary attention without neglecting others.
Whether you're a full-time adventurer or a seasoned warrior currently employed elsewhere, the concept of the Daily Grind

remains the same. The only difference is how much time you can dedicate to each task. While some warriors might tackle all facets of the grind daily, others might spread them strategically throughout the week. The following example serves as a starting point for your personalized Daily Grind – feel free to adapt it to your specific circumstances.

The first rays of dawn paint the sky, marking the start of your daily expedition. The first order of business is a dedicated foray into the bustling online job boards – your digital recruitment outposts teeming with potential opportunities. Dedicate a designated amount of time (1–2 hours) to actively searching for new listings that align with your skills and aspirations. Don't be afraid to explore various job boards – cast a wide net to maximize your chances of encountering the perfect opportunity.

As the sun climbs high, it's time to check in on your progress. Think of your in-game inbox as your war council tent, where you receive critical updates and assess the situation. Has an interview request arrived from a potential employer? Have HR representatives sent messages regarding your application? These notifications are your war cries, urging you to spring into action. Diligently check all in-game notifications (emails, app alerts) throughout the day to stay informed of new job postings that might have slipped your initial notice. If your inbox remains quiet regarding interviews, don't despair! There are tactics to maximize your chances:

- **Email Notifications:** Like job search alerts, enable email notifications on your preferred job boards. These notifications ensure you receive immediate updates about exciting new opportunities.

- **Mobile App Job Search Alerts:** Take advantage of the built-in alert systems that many mobile job search apps offer. These alerts act as virtual scouts, continuously scanning the job market and notifying you about new listings that meet your desired criteria.

Remember, the hero who acts swiftly and decisively is the hero who triumphs. Responding promptly to new job postings and interview requests demonstrates your enthusiasm and commitment.

If the digital sun begins to set and a triumphant fanfare doesn't blare through your speakers, fret not, adventurer! Remember, the hero's journey is rarely linear. Step away from your inbox while you continue your daily grind, dedicating some of your after-hours to interview preparation or delving deeper into open-source contributions on GitHub. You'll recheck it tomorrow. During this continuous improvement time, set your focus on your training and contributions. Polish your resume if it needs an update. There's always room for improvement, and the development city rewards those who continuously hone their craft, just like a skilled warrior sharpens their weapon daily to maintain its sharpness and effectiveness.

Don't forget to combine your entertainment and free time with networking! The digital world offers a vast wilderness of online communities, bustling with fellow adventurers seeking camaraderie and opportunity. After your evening skirmishes with code (or interview prep), consider venturing into these online landscapes – subreddits dedicated to software development, Discord servers teeming with passionate developers – and reach out to your network for referrals. Think of these online communities as virtual campfires where you can swap stories, learn from each other's experiences, build lasting connections, and unearth hidden opportunities. By leveraging your network, both online and offline, you can significantly increase your chances of finding a job that's a good fit for you.

However, internal enemies such as procrastination and lack of motivation can be just as detrimental to progress as any external obstacle. Recognizing these enemies and developing strategies to overcome them is crucial. We will be discussing this in detail in the upcoming chapter.

FUELLING YOUR JOB
SEARCH FIRE

T he echoing cheers of the arena gradually subside, leaving you standing amidst the dust and sweat of countless battles. The coliseum floor is littered with fallen warriors – victims of their own surrender to despair. The job hunt is no different. Slowing down and succumbing to procrastination is akin to laying down your weapons and yielding to defeat. Your muscles ache, your mind races and a sense of accomplishment fills your heart. You've survived another day in the gladiatorial arena of the job hunt. Still, you know that the war is far from over. The daily grind can be relentless, with a constant barrage of applications, rejections, and the ever-present threat of burnout. How do you keep your spirits high and your motivation burning in the face of such adversity?

The answer, my fellow adventurer, lies in the power of ritual and routine. Remember Maximus, the fallen general in Gladiator? Before each battle, he would kneel and touch the earth, grounding himself in the present moment and drawing strength from the memory of his loved ones. You, too, can create a pre-job search ritual, a sacred practice that ignites your fighting spirit and reminds you of what you're fighting for.

It could be a morning meditation, a few minutes of deep breathing, and visualization to center yourself and set your intentions for the day. Or it could be a power playlist, a carefully curated selection of songs that pump you up and get your adrenaline flowing. Whatever your ritual, make it yours, a personal touchstone you can turn to when the going gets tough.

During this secret practice, remind yourself why you're on this quest. What can you bring to the world? How can you make an impact? You need skills to grow, and to grow, you need this job. Remember now and forever: Work to learn, not just to earn. Growth is the path to making a difference.

Music can be your greatest companion in this process; choose an album, an artist or playlist that can fuel determination within you. It's an invisible weapon that empowers you when doubts are present. Use this imaginary soundtrack of growth. Your mission becomes thrilling as if chasing an opportunity through the city streets of code, accompanied by soaring melodies and great beats.

But remember to care for your physical vessel. Your body is your temple, your chariot in this race to success. A daily dose of exercise, whether a brisk walk, a yoga session, or a full-blown workout, can do wonders for your mental and physical well-being. It releases endorphins, reduces stress, and sharpens your focus. Think of it as training for battle, preparing your body and mind for the challenges ahead.

The job hunt can be a tedious grind, but it doesn't have to be joyless. Embrace the power of gamification, turning your daily tasks into a series of challenges and rewards. Set goals for yourself, track your progress and celebrate your achievements, no matter how small. Each application you submit and each interview you ace is a step closer to your ultimate goal.

And remember, even the most hardened warriors need rest. Don't burn yourself out by working around the clock. Make time for sleep, relaxation, and activities that bring you joy. A well-rested mind is a sharp mind better equipped to tackle the challenges of the job hunt. Think of it as restoring your health points and preparing yourself for the subsequent encounter.

Amidst the excitement of the chase lingers a nagging question: What if the rejections persist? What if self-doubt creeps in? These whispers of imposter syndrome tell you that you aren't good enough. However, don't listen to these lies. Even the most successful developers have faced rejection; it's part of the journey and tests your resilience. In the next chapter, we'll create a powerful tool – a personal contract with yourself – to help you stay focused and motivated on your quest for that dream job in Software Development.

The journey to your dream job may be fraught with obstacles, but with the right mindset and the right tools, you can emerge victorious. The gladiatorial arena of the job hunt awaits the adventurer. Are you ready to face your fears and claim your destiny?

FORGING YOUR PACT
WITH SUCCESS

With all its applications and interviews, the job hunt can be thrilling and draining. Victory requires not just skills and talent, but unwavering dedication. Your pre-battle ritual is the start of the fight against procrastination. We are transforming initial motivation into consistent action: you will create a Self-Motivation Contract.

Imagine an ancient scroll, its words illuminated by candlelight, unfurling before you. This is your personal pact – a declaration of your commitment to landing your dream job. Inscribe your aspirations to it. Describe the life you want to achieve and the influence you aim for. This statement of intent will guide you through the trials ahead and serve as a constant reminder of why you chose this harrowing journey in the first place.

Next, outline your skill tree, detailing the areas for growth. How will you master the perfect resume or interview techniques? Are there technologies to conquer or unlock abilities that can transform you into a valuable opponent in Software Development?

A plan guides the battle, like a rudder for a ship. Let your Contract specify goals for the upcoming days and weeks. What results do you need? How much time will be devoted to skill development? Smaller objectives create the momentum to drive your progress.

True champions take responsibility. Use your Self-Motivation Contract to help with this aim by including penalties for falling short on goals – perhaps with additional hours on the task. Such strategies create a more disciplined approach.

Even heroes need rest. Let the Contract clarify that this rest and recovery are essential to achieving this journey to victory: include rewards for your efforts, favorite activities, and quality time with your loved one to restore for challenges that await you tomorrow.

The competition environment is always changing, so regularly review your Contract for shifts. Changing goals isn't a weakness; it highlights your adaptability toward your target. Just like your banner in the wind, let your Contract remind you to stay committed and inspire action during tough times.

Share your goals publicly. Social pressure can drive success by making goals tangible. I strive harder to avoid the shame of unmet targets, which also promotes morale. Focus on developing assertiveness, refining skills, and overcoming obstacles; let self-improvement guide you through challenges.

The Contract is a key to unlock your inner strength and change habits with a well-written statement that guides your journey. Place this personal pact first and master its essence daily, knowing victory is near. You will feel a clear direction after completing this step.

The upcoming stages will teach you techniques for navigating job interviews and processes that arise when your application gains traction, elevating your game. But first, like any gladiator, be prepared to die.

YOU DIED

With your self-motivation contract in hand, you're ready to tackle the job search challenges. But what lies beyond the arena gates? The answer involves embracing a gamer's approach to failure: strategic failure.

When you die in the game, it's not over; you can restart and respawn with new insights. Similarly, in the interview arena, rejections are not the end but an opportunity for growth.

Think of your early interviews as training bouts or the initial levels of a game where you're still learning. They help you get accustomed to the interview format, hone your communication skills, and think on your feet. Like mastering game controls through repeated play, these interviews allow you to refine your answers and gain the composure needed to excel.

If a technical question caught you off guard, it's a signal to level up in that area. If a behavioral question leaves room for improvement, it's time to improve your communication. These interviews reveal your weaknesses, like low stats in a character sheet that need boosting. By reflecting on your performance, you can pinpoint where to focus your learning, emerging stronger for the next challenge.

Pay attention to the interviewer's style, the questions they ask, and the interview's structure – it's like studying a boss's patterns in a game. Reflect on what went well and what didn't, using feedback, or the lack thereof, to your advantage.

The more interviews you undertake, the more adept and confident you become, akin to leveling up your character. The initial anxiety will give way to the poise of a seasoned player, ready for the final boss.

Not every interview will end in triumph, but each one is a learning experience. The "worst" outcome is simply not getting the job, like seeing a game over the screen. But you'll respawn, now wiser, with a better grasp of your strengths and weaknesses, and the resilience of a true warrior.

Remember, there's no absolute failure in the interview arena, only steps toward your ultimate victory – your dream job. Embrace this mindset, learn from every encounter, and you'll move closer to becoming a champion in the world of software development.

Now, with a strong self-motivation and an understanding of strategic failure, you're set to face your first recruiter call, where your preparation will be put to the test.

GLADIATOR'S WELLNESS ASSESSMENT

Bearing in mind the significance of missteps in the interview process, you are now ready to face recruiters and HR representatives. Just as a gladiator undergoes a wellness assessment before entering the arena, you too will be scrutinized during the phone screen, a crucial step in your journey. The path to your dream job may involve submitting numerous applications before reaching this point. But with the right knowledge and a positive mindset, you'll be ready to conquer this challenge.

Consider the phone screen an initial test for the recruiter to assess your battle readiness. Their goals are to confirm your qualifications match the job's requirements and evaluate your interest in the role and company. Why should they be excited about your joining if you seem uninterested? Let's be honest: while gladiators were slaves fighting for survival, we fight for less dramatic reasons, such as paying rent and bills. The recruiter seeks a warrior with genuine enthusiasm and commitment, or at least a convincing attitude performance.

No gladiator enters the arena without studying their opponent. The same principle applies to the phone screen. Before the call, research the company and the specific position you're applying for. Review the job description meticulously, paying close attention to the required skills and experience. Visit the company website, delve into their social media presence, and glean any insights about their work culture and values. This knowledge empowers you to confidently discuss your alignment with the position and the company.

Like a gladiator raising their sword in salute, your opening is critical. Project professionalism and unwavering enthusiasm from the very first "hello." Speak clearly and concisely, ensuring your voice conveys confidence and a genuine interest in the conversation. Remember, first impressions are lasting impressions – this initial phone call sets the tone for the rest of the interview process.

The recruiter will likely ask standard questions during the phone screen. Prepare to discuss your experience, skills, and motivation for applying. View these questions as predictable attacks you can parry. Practice concise responses that highlight your relevant qualifications and enthusiasm for the role. For instance, if asked about a specific technology, don't just say you lack experience; explain how you've been learning through open-source projects. Mention helpful projects and your work with tutorials and documentation to build your understanding. Even without years of professional experience, showing your initiative and eagerness to learn can attract potential employers.

The recruiter's *"Tell me about yourself and your interest in this position"* question is critical to unlocking your gladiator potential. Show your motivation towards a specific development field, mention relevant technologies that make you thrive with opportunities that excite you, and connect those dots with the current role that you are pursuing. For example, showcase skills acquired on open source, the experience learned through personal dedication and other actions made outside typical work structure. This would resonate as a unique trait in a competitive environment, showing them why you're not just another job seeker and how all the skills you've learned there have shaped your experience.

If the interviewer asks: *"Why do you wish to be a part of our company,"* you must demonstrate knowledge about their purpose and goals. Align those aspects to your professional learning needs, demonstrating a shared vision in values or approaches. Even if it's just about how those technologies used in that company will create the desired outcomes that might empower them to grow professionally. All those details demonstrate a well-deserved position in their teams because what you wish to achieve matches goals and projects with potential influence.

Show honesty in weaker aspects; interviewers expect little from juniors, making it a chance to demonstrate self-awareness over skills. Always articulate these wisely, reflecting an understanding of the role. For example, if lack of testing knowledge is raised, highlight areas for growth, as little is needed initially. This indicates a willingness to improve. Choose minor flaws over major weaknesses – this requires experience and should remain a strategic approach in professional settings.

In a competitive arena, gladiators were evaluated on their physical prowess, combat skills, and endurance. Victorious gladiators stood out by overcoming technical challenges. They had to think quickly and adapt strategies when faced with formidable opponents or unexpected obstacles. This skill is crucial today, where problem-solving and adaptability are key for success. Recruiters seek candidates who demonstrate these abilities. When asked, *"Tell me about a time you faced a technical challenge. How did you overcome it?"* provide a clear, engaging answer that showcases your problem-solving skills and adaptability setbacks.

Remember, the phone screen is a two-way street. While the recruiter assesses you, you also have the opportunity to showcase your value. Don't wait passively for questions. Look for opportunities to connect your skills and experiences to the specific needs of the role, as outlined in the job description. This proactive approach demonstrates your initiative and genuine interest in the position.

Skilled gladiator doesn't simply react to their opponent's attacks; they take the initiative. The phone screen offers a similar opportunity. Prepare a list of well-researched questions for the recruiter. Inquire about the team structure, the day-to-day responsibilities of the role, or the company's culture. Thoughtful questions demonstrate your genuine interest in the position and desire to learn more about the company.

Discussing salary expectations can be a sensitive topic. If it comes up, remember that the purpose of this question at the initial stage is often to filter candidates out of the hiring process. Do your research and find out the typical salary ranges for these positions. Instead of providing a specific number, offer a range to give yourself some flexibility. Like a gladiator in the arena, don't let them corner you with no room to maneuver. Understand the standard compensation for similar roles in your industry and location beforehand. Keep in mind that you can always negotiate the details later in the process.

Even the most seasoned gladiator can make mistakes. During the phone screen, avoid rambling or negativity. Be prepared to answer questions concisely and with enthusiasm. Speak well of previous employers, if any, and discuss relevant topics. Maintain a professional demeanor throughout the call.

With this knowledge and the right battle plan, you can conquer the phone screen wellness assessment and advance to the next stage of the interview arena – the coding challenge.

WIELDING YOUR WEAPON IN THE ARENA

Having successfully navigated the gatekeeper's scrutiny during the phone screen, you're now about to engage in the real test of your skills – the coding challenge. Envision this as the crux of the interview arena, where you'll showcase your coding prowess, much like a gladiator displaying their mastery in combat.

The coding challenge is designed to assess your ability to handle the core weapon of your trade – code. Here, the spotlight is entirely on your technical skills and your capacity to solve problems. As judges, senior developers will evaluate your proficiency in implementing algorithms and data structures and your ability to write clean, efficient, and well-structured code, reflecting your craftsmanship.

The format of this challenge can vary much like different combat styles in the Coliseum. You might be asked to solve problems on a whiteboard, on paper, or through an online coding platform. Sometimes, it could be a take-home coding challenge, or you might need to code during a call with an interviewer. The medium changes, but the goal remains: demonstrate your ability to think critically and translate problems into effective code.

Common themes in these challenges include solving problems related to fundamental data types such as arrays and strings, as well as data structures like graphs and hash maps. These challenges assess your ability to manipulate data effectively and demonstrate a strong understanding of algorithmic problem-solving. You may also be asked to analyze the complexity[110] of your solutions, showcasing your grasp of code optimization. Studying everything overnight is unrealistic; it will be difficult and somewhat dependent on luck.

However, remember that recruiters from third-party agencies are genuinely invested in your success – they earn their pay when you succeed in this arena. Essentially, they've placed a bet on your victory. Feel free to ask about typical tasks from the target company during the upcoming tech challenge. Previous participants who weren't fortunate enough to pass their challenges may have shared useful information. However, this approach won't work with the employer's in-house HR team. Avoid trying to engage in this tactic with them as it could lead to penalties and disqualification from the arena.

Preparation is crucial, much like how a gladiator practices their moves. Utilize platforms such as LeetCode[111] and HackerRank[112] to tackle various problems designed for interview scenarios. Aim to solve as many tasks as possible on these platforms, especially if you receive a hint from the gatekeeper about which tasks might be on the horizon. This step is vital because, without a formal degree where theoretical knowledge is taught, your experience primarily stems from open-source contributions, which is very practical and lacks the theoretical grounding needed here. It may seem somewhat absurd that the hiring process and tasks are structured this way. Coding challenges often rely on theoretical knowledge

---

[110] https://www.geeksforgeeks.org/analysis-algorithms-big-o-analysis/
[111] https://leetcode.com/
[112] https://www.hackerrank.com/

that is seldom utilized in everyday commercial applications. You're unlikely to apply this knowledge in your daily job. Most likely, you'll only encounter these puzzles again when you decide to switch jobs and face yet another series of seemingly pointless riddles from the next employer.

A MULTI-FACETED ARENA CLASH

Y ou stand triumphant, your metaphorical sword (your coding skills) gleaming in the arena sun. But the path to securing your dream developer job continues! Now, you face the ultimate challenge – the technical interview. This high-intensity battle
tests your programming prowess across a broad spectrum. In this
gladiatorial spectacle, not just your swordsmanship but your tacti-
cal thinking, communication skills, and overall knowledge are put
to the final test.

While the coding challenge focused on your ability to wield
your coding weapon, the technical interview expanded the battlefield. Here, you'll be evaluated on a broader range of skills,
demonstrating your understanding of software development principles, problem-solving approach, and ability to communicate
complex technical concepts clearly. Imagine this interview as a series of intricate maneuvers – parrying questions about algorithms
with a well-reasoned explanation and delivering a well-aimed
counterattack with a thoughtful solution to a design problem.

Just as you hone your coding skills through online platforms,
you also need to train your theoretical knowledge. The open-

source community once again provides a valuable resource – the Awesome Interviews repository (Screenshot 31). This meticulously curated collection is a virtual armory stocked with various technical interview questions categorized by multiple programming languages, frameworks, platforms, and even database and operating system technologies.

Screenshot 31: Awesome Interviews GitHub project.
https://github.com/DopplerHQ/awesome-interview-questions

The Awesome Interviews repository thrives on the collective knowledge of the developer community. Delve into the depths of the Awesome Interviews repository, and you will discover a wealth of knowledge specifically crafted to get you ready for the technical interview.

You can utilize this invaluable resource to prepare for your battles and are encouraged to contribute your experiences and insights. Explore sections dedicated to your preferred programming languages, the frameworks you've mastered, and even the database technologies relevant to your dream position. Each section offers a comprehensive list of potential interview questions, empowering you to anticipate challenges and formulate well-reasoned responses.

This repository's immense popularity, with over 70,000 stars, 1,700 watchers, and 8,500 forks, underscores the power of the open-source community. By leveraging this shared knowledge base, you'll enter the technical interview arena well-equipped and prepared to face any challenge the interviewers throw your way.

THE COLISEUM CROWD

Y ou stand in the crowd's applause, representing the company you're interviewing with. But the battle isn't over! Just as a gladiator's fate isn't solely determined by skill, your success depends on your ability to engage with the audience. This next challenge focuses on your soft skills: communication, problem-solving, and cultural fit. Imagine yourself not as a lone gladiator but as a captivating orator, winning over the crowd to secure your dream job in Software Development.

Think of the cultural fit interview like speaking to a large crowd in a coliseum. Instead of just talking to one person, you will have conversations with several interviewers at once. In this social setting, you need to understand how groups work and share your skills and experiences with many people. Your communication skills are very important here. You need to express your thoughts clearly, listen to their questions, and show the excitement that everyone can feel. Imagine it as giving several short speeches to the crowd, where each one can change their opinion about you.

Here are six common questions for cultural fit interviews and strategies to highlight your open-source experience for a commercial development role. Don't downplay your contributions;

instead, present them as valuable training that equips you with essential skills for success in a commercial environment setting.

- *"Describe your ideal work environment."* Express enjoyment in the collaborative nature of open-source projects but emphasize a desire to shift to a focused, product-driven development environment. You could say, *"I love the problem-solving of open source, but I'm ready to apply that to impactful products with closer team collaboration."*

- *"Describe a time you went above and beyond for a project."* Describe a significant feature you championed or a crucial bug you resolved in an open-source project, showcasing your dedication and work ethic. Then, convey your enthusiasm for taking ownership of features in a commercial setting, where your contributions influence the product's success directly.

- *"How do you handle constructive criticism?"* Describe how code reviews in open-source projects refined your skills as a developer. For example, *"Open source taught me to see feedback as a learning opportunity. I look forward to structured mentorship and code reviews in a commercial environment to continuously improve."*

- *"Tell me about a time you failed and what you learned."* Cite an open-source project where your initial approach failed. Highlight your debugging process and how you redefined the problem, then convey your eagerness to apply these lessons in a commercial setting to benefit the entire team.

- *"What are you looking for in your next role?"* Discuss your aim to create impactful products for users. Emphasize your eagerness to learn best practices, support the team's success, and grow with experienced mentors.

- *"Tell me about a time you've disagreed with a technical approach. How did you handle it?"* Share a time you suggested an alternative approach in an open-source project. Explain how you researched solutions, presented your idea logically, and collaborated to find a compromise or enhanced solution.

Your open-source experience highlights your technical skills, collaboration, and problem-solving. Emphasize how it prepares you for commercial development. By viewing open source as a training ground and showing your readiness to join a focused team, you distinguish yourself and boost your chances of landing your dream job.

Your path was uncertain, but you were now more experienced than ever before. You became a strong communicator and a vital contributor, ready to share your talents with a team that values your passion.

The final chapter of your job-seeking journey was about to begin. In the next chapter, we will embark on the final challenge – the boss fight!

FINAL BOSS FIGHT

T he Coliseum crowd roars as you defeat the tech trivia trolls and coding goblins. Each challenge conquered brings you closer to the final boss: The Interview with the Emperor. You're not just a skilled fighter; you're a charismatic orator, having honed your skills rallying fellow grinders in forums and open-source communities. You can inspire and motivate, and you're confident you can use those powers to impress the Emperor.

Remember those soul-crushing rejections? The vicious cycle of needing experience to get experience? The endless quest for the mythical level 70, a cruel gatekeeping hurdle erected by HR overlords to filter out worthy novices from the masses? The Emperor, the ultimate decision-maker, is the embodiment of that system. A mysterious person, his reputation is known by many. Some say he is an experienced tech expert, wise from years of work. Others describe him as a young genius who figured out how to be successful before becoming an adult. Love him or hate him. You have to respect the empire he's built. And you are about to storm his castle.

The Game Over screen of your past failures flashes before your eyes. Your heart pounds like a drum solo, a symphony of imposter syndrome. "I shouldn't be here," you think. "I'm a fraud, a glitch in the system."

But then you remember the countless nights spent grinding away at conversations with AI about coding concepts, countless traffic lights turning green, and the communities you've rallied. You aren't an imposter. You are a warrior, forged in the fires of determination and fueled by the unwavering belief that you belong in this arena.

The heavy wooden doors swing open, revealing the Emperor's quarters. Sunlight streams through stained-glass windows, illuminating a grand chamber filled with intricate tapestries and gleaming suits of armor. The Emperor sits on a massive throne, his eyes fixed on you as you enter.

"Welcome, challenger," the Emperor greets you, his voice smooth as polished chrome. "Come closer. Let us speak as equals."

A wave of warmth washes over you as the Emperor gestures for you to take a seat. He leans forward, his piercing gaze locking onto yours.

"Tell me, warrior," he begins, his voice low and rumbling. What drives you? What fuels your ambition?"

You take a deep breath, summoning the courage you've honed throughout your journey. "Your Majesty," you begin, your voice steady and clear, "I am driven by a passion for creation, a thirst for knowledge, and an unwavering belief in the power of collaboration. I see technology not as a mere tool, but as a force for good, a catalyst for positive change."

You speak of your open-source conquests, lessons learned from failure, and the burning desire to build a better world. You share your vision for the future, a world where technology empowers individuals, fosters connection, and unlocks human potential.

The Emperor listens intently, a subtle smile playing on his lips. He nods occasionally, his eyes sparkling with a mixture of curiosity and admiration.

"You speak with the fire of a true warrior," he says. "But tell me, what makes you think you have what it takes to join my guard?"

This is your chance to turn the tables and show you aren't just a passive player but an active participant in the game. You've researched and studied the company's history, products, and culture. You ask insightful questions, probing for the deeper meaning behind their mission, challenges, and aspirations.

The Emperor is impressed. He shares his insights, vision for the future, and the impact he hopes you can make. It is a conversation, not an interrogation, a meeting of minds rather than a clash of egos.

As the conversation draws close, a comfortable silence fills the chamber. The Emperor reclines on his throne, his eyes sparkling with amusement. "Thank you, warrior," he says. "You've given me much to consider. We'll be in touch soon."

You rise from your seat, a sense of accomplishment washing over you. You've faced your fears, conquered your doubts, and emerged more robust on the other side. You've shown the Emperor that you are more than just a line on a resume, more than just a score on a leaderboard. You are a force to be reckoned with.

The Emperor's words echo in your mind as you step back out into the bustling city. You exhale a sigh of relief. You've done it. You've survived the final boss battle. Now, all that is left is to wait for the victory fanfare. But even if the Emperor doesn't offer you a place in his guard, you know you've won something far more valuable: the confidence to face any challenge, the knowledge that you can level up and achieve your dreams.

As you stroll through the city, the familiar magical cat – your trusty Quest Helper – glides beside you. There's no need for greetings between you; the connection is palpable as if he has been by your side all along, just waiting for the moment to reveal himself. Like a true feline friend, he's been silently watching over you, invisible yet always present.

The bond you share is a comforting silence, a deep understanding born from facing challenges together. His presence is a gentle reminder that, no matter how daunting the journey may seem, you are never truly alone. Together, you navigate these bustling streets one last time, ready to embrace whatever adventures lie ahead.

THE NEW CHAPTER

D o you remember first chapters?" Quest Helper purrs, weaving between your legs. "When you were a lost passenger, overwhelmed by the endless education options?" The cat's tail swishes as he guides you through the memories of your journey, reminding you of the transformation from a passenger to a driver, the confidence gained as you chose your open-source project and your electric scooter, navigating the winding roads of code. "You've battled your way through the gladiatorial arena of job hunting," he continues, "honing your skills and proving your worth."

The cat pauses, his whiskers twitching, his light flickering as he contemplates your next move. "This is the end of our game together, but the start of a new chapter in your life. The path ahead is yours to choose."

He paints a vivid picture of the possibilities that lie before you. Will you continue fighting in the gladiatorial arena, seeking new challenges and opportunities? Or will you discover that this path isn't for you, that the thrill of the battle doesn't outweigh the cost?

Quest Helper assures you, "Both endings are wonderful. The Software Development City isn't for everyone. It's a demanding world filled with challenges and setbacks. But it's also a world of immense opportunity, where you can build a fulfilling career, make a real impact, and create something significant."

As the cat's words sink in, a familiar figure steps forward from the shadows – Dan, the owner of Quest Helper. He smiles warmly, his eyes filled with pride and hope.

"Hey there, adventurer," he begins, his voice a comforting rumble. "We've been honored to accompany you on this journey. It's been an extraordinary adventure, hasn't it? Can you honestly say you've ever experienced anything quite like it?"

Dan pauses, allowing his words to resonate. "The open-source path, the AI-powered tools we've utilized... this is a brave new world we're venturing into, a world where the traditional barriers to entry are crumbling. It's a world where anyone with passion, dedication, and a willingness to learn can carve their own path."

Quest Helper hops onto Dan's shoulder, giving him a playful nip. "Ow! See, he's still got some bite," Dan chuckles, rubbing the spot where the cat bit him. "If this unconventional guide has been valuable to you and helped you level up and gain a deeper under-standing of the software development landscape, I have a small request. Perhaps you could consider sharing your experience in your review[113]? Your words could be a guiding light for others who are just starting their journeys. It would mean the world to me."

Dan's smile widens as he continues, "Regardless of where your path leads, remember the timeless wisdom: *'The true meaning of life is to plant trees under whose shade you do not expect to sit.'* Find your purpose, nurture your passion, and leave a legacy that will outlive you."

Quest Helper rubs against your leg one last time, purring softly. As he speaks, he starts to glow brighter. "You've come so far, and I'm proud of you," he says, his voice softening. "I've en-joyed every moment of our journey together. But it's time for you to take the next steps on your own." With a final affectionate

---

[113] https://greenlightcareer.tech/book/review

nuzzle, he begins to fade away, his light dimming gently until he disappears.

Dan watches with a gentle smile, then looks back at you, giving you a nod. "This isn't farewell," he says. "Stay in touch[114]. I have more to share, and who knows? Maybe Quest Helper will make a return."

With that, Dan leaves you alone in the digital void. The screen fades to black, and the gentle hum of your computer fills the silence. Suddenly, pixelated green letters materialize against the darkness:

GAME OVER

CONTINUE? [Y/n]

The cursor blinks expectantly, but before you can respond, the pixels begin to blur and swirl. The green glow intensifies, expanding until it engulfs your vision entirely. The digital hum crescendos into a cacophony of beeps and whirs, then abruptly shifts to a singular, steady tone.

The steady beep of a heart monitor pierces through the haze, pulling you back from the brink. Your eyelids flutter, heavy as lead, struggling against the harsh fluorescent light above. The acrid smell of antiseptic burns your nostrils, grounding you in a reality that feels both familiar and alien.

"Where am I? What happened?" The questions swirl in your mind, but you can't voice them.

Your throat constricts, raw and dehydrated. You try to speak, but only a weak rasp escapes your lips. A cool hand touches your arm, and a blurry figure leans into view.

"Easy now," a gentle voice soothes. "You've been through quite an ordeal."

As your vision clears, you recognize the crisp white coat of a doctor. The events leading up to this moment come rushing back

---

[114] https://greenlightcareer.tech/book/stayintouch

in a dizzying flood: the car accident, the screeching of brakes, the sickening crunch of metal, and then... darkness.

But something else lingers at the edges of your consciousness. A dream? No, more than that. A journey. A city of code and possibility. The weight of an electric scooter beneath you as you navigated winding streets of algorithms. The comforting presence of a glowing cat named Quest Helper. And through it all, a persistent green light is guiding your way.

The doctor's voice cuts through your reverie. "We almost lost you," she says, her tone a mixture of relief and lingering concern. "But you fought your way back. It's nothing short of miraculous."

You try to sit up, wincing at the protest of sore muscles. "I saw... a green light," you manage to croak out. "It was everywhere, leading me through a strange city."

The doctor's expression softens with understanding. "Ah, yes. Many patients report vivid experiences during their time in a coma. What you experienced were likely hallucinations."

She pulls up a chair, her demeanor shifting from clinical to compassionate. "Hallucinations can occur during a coma, especially in medically induced cases like yours. They're often a result of the powerful medications we use and the severity of the illness or injury. These experiences can feel incredibly real and meaningful to patients."

You nod slowly, processing this information. "But it felt so... transformative. I learned so much about software development, about myself."

The doctor smiles gently. "The mind is a powerful thing. Even in unconsciousness, it can create rich, complex narratives. These experiences, while not literally real, can profoundly impact a person's psyche and outlook."

The words hang in the air, crackling with possibility. The heart monitor's steady beep seems to quicken, matching the surge of determination coursing through you.

The doctor's expression warms. "Well," she says, "it seems you've been given a second chance. These experiences, whether hallucinations or not, clearly hold great meaning for you. Make the most of this opportunity."

As she turns to leave, you catch a glimpse of something impossible – a faint, familiar green glow beneath the door. It disappears in an instant, leaving you to wonder if it was ever there at all.

You close your eyes, recalling the vivid journey through Software Development City. The lessons learned, the confidence gained, and the skills acquired all feel viscerally real, etched into your very being.

The heart monitor's steady rhythm becomes a countdown, marking the seconds until your new life truly begins.

Beep. Beep. Beep.

A chill runs down your spine, equal parts excitement and trepidation. You open your mouth to speak, surprised to find your voice stronger than expected.

"I... I think I know what I need to do now."

The doctor raises an eyebrow, clearly intrigued. "Oh? And what's that?"

You take a deep breath, feeling the weight of this moment. It's as if you're standing at a crossroads, the path ahead suddenly illuminated by that persistent green glow from your vision.

"I'm going to become a software developer."

Printed in Great Britain
by Amazon

58872702R00119